you can

stop

humming

now

you can

stop

humming

now

A DOCTOR'S STORIES OF
LIFE, DEATH AND IN BETWEEN

DANIELA LAMAS

piatkus

PIATKUS

First published in the US in 2018 by Little, Brown and Company
First published in Great Britain in 2018 by Piatkus

1 3 5 7 9 10 8 6 4 2

Several of these pieces have appeared, in different form, in the *New York Times*
and at newyorker.com. Excerpt from "Stepping Stones" by Rachel Hadas © 2016 by
TriQuarterly Books/Northwestern University Press. Published 2016 by TriQuarterly
Books/Northwestern University Press. All rights reserved. Reprinted with permission.

A CIP catalogue record for this book
is available from the British Library.

ISBN 978-0-349-41277-1

Printed and bound in Great Britain by
Clays Ltd, St Ives plc

Papers used by Piatkus are from well-managed forests
and other responsible sources.

Piatkus
An imprint of
Little, Brown Book Group
Carmelite House
50 Victoria Embankment
London EC4Y 0DZ

An Hachette UK Company
www.hachette.co.uk

www.littlebrown.co.uk

For my mother

Note

This account is based on both my clinical practice and my independent reporting. Certain names and identifying details, including those for all of my patients, have been changed. In a few instances I have created composites to best convey my experiences and conclusions.

Contents

What else can I bring?
I'm carrying my story,
this much-crumpled thing.
What else can I bring,
what humble offering
served as allegory?
What else can I bring?
I'm carrying my story.

—Rachel Hadas, "Stepping Stones"

you can

stop

humming

now

Introduction

Nearly a decade has passed since my first night in the intensive care unit. Though some of the details have faded, I can still remember my fear, my heart racing and arms burning as I compressed a chest at the first code, and then, in the morning, before exhaustion overtook me, the knowledge that I'd found what I wanted to do. At first, I just hoped to learn the medicine, to recognize every potential presentation of a rare disease, abnormal lab value, and unusual physical exam finding. I saw family members at the bedside, but I did not let myself feel the fear and worry that rolled off them in waves. In truth, throughout the whole of my internal medicine residency, I barely paused.

Instead, I became the resident who didn't let anyone die. People knew this. I was proud of it, and in many ways, I still am. Back then, it felt as though my job was to do whatever I could to keep a heart beating, whether that was another procedure, or medication to support failing blood pressure, or a stat page to anesthesia for an intubation, or a nick and a dilator and pressure and a catheter in the neck and an early morning call to the kidney doctors to start a patient on dialysis. When I talked to families during those harried days and nights, I didn't ask questions. What was there to ask? I made declarations. "We're doing the best we can," I would say. I hoped that it was true. I wanted to do the right thing, and this was the way I knew how. "We're doing everything."

The technology blazed so bright that I could barely see beyond it. There were the standard advances I knew about but had never witnessed up close, like breathing machines for the lungs and dialysis to take the place of the kidneys, and the awe-inspiring idea that surgeons could cut an organ out of one person and sew it into another. Extracorporeal membrane oxygenation took damaged lungs out of the equation entirely by sucking blood from a patient's body and running it through a machine that added oxygen and removed carbon dioxide. Those with diseases that decades ago would have killed them in childhood could outlive their life expectancies. To think that I could be a part of all that was remarkable.

But during those same years—so quietly that at first I barely noticed—something else crept in. As a second-year resident, I cared for an old man with severe anemia from recurrent bouts of bloody diarrhea. Specialists tried again and again to find out where in his intestines the blood was coming from. They scoped and they cauterized and they clipped, and yet day after day, my patient's

4

counts dropped. We ordered more blood transfusions, and still he grew weaker. Each morning I entered his room and leaned over his bed to place my stethoscope on his chest, and when I had finished listening, he would look up at me and ask if he could leave the hospital yet. I'd tell him he could not, because he had not stopped bleeding. He would nod and it seemed that he understood, but the next morning, he would ask the same question again. I would give him the same answer and tell him that I hoped it would be soon.

The days went by until one morning, my patient told me that he was done. *You can't be done,* I thought. *You're still bleeding*. But that didn't matter to him. He didn't want us to keep talking about new procedures and ordering blood transfusions. His arms were bruised from needle sticks. Every time we gave him a transfusion, his lungs filled with fluid and he felt as though he were drowning until we gave him another medicine to make him urinate so that he could breathe again. He was ninety years old, and he was only getting weaker in the hospital, not better. Even though I knew that, even though I felt a little nervous and guilty when I saw him each morning, I found his words unexpected and somehow insulting. So I tried to negotiate. I told him that I was sorry we had kept him from eating for so many nights, awaiting procedures that inevitably occurred late in the day and sometimes not at all. I could bring him some food from the cafeteria, I offered, anything he wanted. I needed him to understand that if he stuck with us a bit longer, then maybe we could make him better.

He didn't want our kind of better. He missed his home and his bed and his television and the way it was quiet at night and the sunlight crept in through his bedroom window each morning. It wasn't the house where he had raised his family, but still he had his chair in the living room and he had his books. So he shook his head no. He didn't want anything from the cafeteria. He just wanted to leave.

Maybe he was depressed. I called the psychiatrists, half hoping that they would tell me he wasn't able to make his own decisions. They spent a long while in his room, and when they emerged they were certain that my patient's mind was entirely sound. He understood the consequences. He understood that he would keep bleeding and slowly become weaker and more anemic, and that eventually he would die from the blood loss. Surprised and frustrated by their determination, I filled out the discharge paperwork that sent him on his way.

I went over our final set of conversations for weeks. The way I saw it, my patient had come in with a problem that we weren't good enough to solve so he had decided to go home, where he would die. It was clear to me that we'd failed. I was surprised when, a few months later, a flower delivery arrived at the nurses' station on one of the general medical floors. There was a vase of lilacs and with it, a note for me. It took me a moment before I registered the name and realized that the flowers were from my patient's son.

Certain I had done something wrong and anxious about what I would find, I opened the envelope. I learned that with the aid of a hospice team, my patient had lived out his final days at home, as was his preference. His son was writing because he wanted to thank the doctors who'd taken care of his father during the last of his many hospitalizations. He had spoken highly of us, it turned out. He knew how hard it had been for us to see him leave, and he was grateful that we had. I read the note again. I think that might have been the first time I'd heard from a patient or his family after a hospital discharge. I know it was the first thanks that I'd received, and all this for a decision that hadn't even been mine to make. I took one of the lilacs with me and pressed it between the pages of the pocket-sized medicine text I kept in my white coat.

The memory of this patient and his son's unexpected gift stayed with me. And as I returned to his story in the coming years, I began to see it in a different light. My elderly patient made the choice to leave the hospital so that he could live the way he wanted, for whatever time he had remaining. Was that a failure, as I had assumed, or a kind of success? What did those words even mean? As I began to look farther down the road, at the longer-term reverberations and repercussions of our decisions, distinctions that had once seemed so clear started to blur.

During those days of negotiation in my patient's room, I had believed survival was all that mattered. Maybe that is the way it must be for doctors at the very beginning.

But survival was just the start. There was an entire range of possibilities and outcomes beyond the stark life-or-death dichotomy. Sitting in outpatient clinic offices and at the bedside on the general medical floors, I found myself wondering what my patients might face after they left my care. I wanted to know how they would learn to adapt to new realities and whether they would regret the decisions they had made, or those that had been made for them.

These are the questions that ultimately fueled the stories in this book. In the years since my first overnight in the intensive care unit, I completed my internship and internal medicine residency and went on to a pulmonary and critical care fellowship. I am now an attending physician in the intensive care unit at the hospital where I was born. In this position, I am the one who makes decisions about diagnoses and courses of treatment, leads family meetings, and carries responsibility for my patients' outcomes. Throughout the course of my training for this role, I have learned how to manage a ventilator, how to treat sepsis, and how to sort out the causes of renal failure. I have even learned to look at death, to be present in that moment when the body stills, and to feel the weight of that ending and not to look away. But what I didn't learn during those same years is what comes after for those who do not die, whose lives are extended by days, months, or even years as a result of cutting-edge treatments and invasive technologies.

As medicine marches ever forward, theirs are essential stories to tell. Men and women with cystic fibrosis navigate adulthoods they never thought they'd live to see, the media-savvy turn to Facebook to look for kidney donors, some survivors of the intensive care unit struggle with post-traumatic stress while others live out their days tethered to ventilators in places called long-term acute care hospitals. Some of the people in this book are patients I cared for as a doctor, others I encountered as a writer. Each of them has been shaken by illness or injury, and none would be alive without the most current medical advances. Thinking about their narratives, it's easy to get caught up in the brilliance and sophistication of medicines and machines, but the quiet moments that resonate with me have little to do with any of that.

What is perhaps most extraordinary about these stories is how ordinary they ultimately are. When we follow these men and women into their worlds, where the outcomes of our acute care decisions are lived, the science starts to fade. We are left simply with people, each of them trying to make their way through the unexpected burdens, trade-offs, and triumphs of survival.

1

You Can Stop Humming Now

Nearly halfway through my first year as a doctor, I became Facebook friends with a young man who was dying in the cardiac intensive care unit.

Sam Newman was twenty-eight years old and his heart was failing. When his doctors realized that he was too sick to be cared for in the New Jersey community hospital close to his home, they had started to make phone calls to surrounding hospitals, hoping to send the young man out to the nearest tertiary care medical center. I'm not sure how long it took for them to find a willing institution with the necessary specialists and an open bed. But what I do know is that one night that winter, an ambulance carried Sam Newman, his fear, and the vague hope of a heart transplant to the cardiac intensive care unit at New York Presbyterian Hospital, where I was in the midst of my cardiac ICU rotation. I had been a doctor for just shy of six months.

I wasn't on call when Sam arrived. I was at home in my apartment, trying to sleep, but failing. I was so tired that year—an anxious kind of tired in which I could doze off despite being squished between strangers in the middle of a crowded subway car and miss my stop, but when I finally got into bed at night, all I could do was toss and turn. Those sleepless nights were so frustrating that I was half relieved when I saw my watch tick toward 5 a.m., because it meant I could officially wake up, get into the shower, and start readying myself for the day. That morning, when I arrived at the hospital, I took my place in the semicircle assembled outside one of the patient rooms to begin our daily ICU rounds. We always started with the sickest or most complicated new admission and finished with the patient who required the least of our waning energy, the person who had been in the unit for days and was simply awaiting a bed on the general medical floor or transfer to a rehab hospital. Sam Newman was both the sickest and the most complicated one on our list that morning, so the room we stood in front of was his.

The bleary-eyed intern who had admitted Sam overnight stood slightly forward, in the middle of the group. A few eager medical students clustered nearby, hoping to have the opportunity to show off what they'd memorized. A perky, well-dressed pharmacist was poised at attention, ready to block our inadvertent attempts to overdose our patients on antibiotics, potassium supplements, or sedatives. I took my place with the rest of the first-year doctors and our second-year supervisors in our uniform of white coats with yellowed collars, T-shirts, and rumpled scrub pants. We faced what seemed to me to be an impossible task of trying simultaneously to listen to our new patient's history, place orders for the meds he'd need throughout the day, field corrections on the meds from the pharmacist, and tune out the noise.

Sometimes the background noise of critical illness was all I could hear. There was the strangely melodic crescendo-decrescendo *do-do-do-do-do* of the ventilator, the rhythmic staccato of heart rate monitors, the whooshing of the Zamboni-like vacuum that seemed programmed to clean the floor during the most emotional moments of a hushed family conversation. Every now and then a nurse would come by and pluck one of us interns away, to clarify a medication order or to transport a patient to a CT scan or even to declare a person dead. The best I could do, most of the time, was to hope I'd absorb the highlights. I'd been a doctor for nearly half a year, and I had almost forgotten what it might be like to hear a person's story in its entirety. In its place, I'd learned to distill each patient into a set of check boxes on a to-do list called the Scut List that we would plod through over the course of the day. There was no before or after; there was just the Scut List and the tasks that we needed to finish before I could go home. Narrative, like full nights of sleep, had faded into memory.

But that day I heard "twenty-eight years old," and the beeping of the ventilators and heart rate monitors, the whooshing of the Zamboni, and the dank smell of human sickness all faded to the background. This patient and I were nearly the same age. And so even though my co-intern launched into our new patient's history in the clipped tones and terse language we'd perfected throughout that summer and fall—"This is a twenty-eight-year-old man who was in his usual state of good health until one year ago, when he developed lower-extremity edema"—I found myself, for what seemed like the first time since medical school, actually listening and creating a story.

Sam Newman was putting in long hours as an investment banker when he started to notice that his ankles were swollen at the end of the day. He wondered if it was because he was spending too much time sitting. Or maybe it was from drinking. With all that stress at work, he had been going at it a little hard. He'd cut down on beer and get back on the basketball court if he ever found the time. But then the swelling got worse. He woke up in the middle of the night, sweaty and gasping for air as if he were suffocating. He had to sit bolt upright before he could breathe again. "His lower-extremity edema increased, newly accompanied by orthopnea," my co-intern recited. Sam thought it might be panic attacks. The job was really getting to him. *He must have been so scared,* I thought as I stood outside his door that morning. A buddy at work told him he was fine and he should stop acting crazy, but gave him the name of a local doctor just in case. Sam waited a few weeks before finally squeezing in an appointment one morning. The internist must have assumed, as I would have, that this young guy with a demanding job was just stressed. He would have heard Sam's story and nodded reassuringly. I imagined how he must have placed the stethoscope against Sam's chest to listen to his lungs, casually at first, the way you do when you know it's fine, fully expecting the lungs to sound clear. But instead of the strong, unencumbered breaths of a young man, he heard a crackling through his stethoscope, like the sound hair makes if you rub it between your fingers. Fluid had filled the lungs' delicate air sacs. The doctor's expression would have changed ever so slightly, his jaw tightening and the room going still.

"Just give me a cough," he might have instructed his patient, still disbelieving, hoping the sounds would clear and things would proceed as he'd expected them to—a quick exam, a healthy young man. Sam coughed. He felt nervous without knowing why. "Is everything okay?" he asked. But his doctor was quiet. He was already listening, his face intense and eyes unreadable as his mind shifted into focus. He leaned down again and felt the legs. The slight swelling, so easy to dismiss moments before, now took on a whole new meaning.

The doctor did not tell Sam the extent of his worry, not at first, because there was no point in upsetting the young man before gathering more information. Sam was scared, too scared to ask questions because he did not even know what he should be afraid of and he didn't want the answers, so their conversation was brief. Sam would get a chest X-ray the same day. When the image came back hazy with fluid that had filled his lungs, Sam returned for an ultrasound of his heart, which revealed that the muscle was beating at only half of the strength predicted. The doctor called Sam with that news and told him he would have to go into the hospital. When he heard Sam's breath quicken on the other end of the line, all he wanted was to reassure his patient, and so the doctor kept talking, filling the silence. He told Sam that it was probably just a virus that had affected his heart, and if that was the case, then it could pass, as viruses do, and Sam would get better. So Sam focused on this idea of a virus and told his boss at work that he would have to take a couple of days off, something about a virus, but that he would be fine. He called his mother, too, and though he spoke in generalities, she understood enough that her stomach sank and her hands shook and she started to cry, even when he told her it was probably just a random virus, that he'd get better soon, and so she shouldn't worry.

He didn't get better. He left the hospital with a set of prescriptions, and his mother bought him a pillbox and brought it over to his apartment. She arranged her adult son's medications by morning and evening for the seven days of the week. Two weeks of meds passed. Then there was a biopsy. Sam lay on the cardiac catheterization table, feet dangling over the edge, cold and scared and uncomfortable. His doctors placed a thick catheter into his neck, into the large internal jugular vein that sits next to the carotid artery. They threaded a smaller catheter with little jaws at the end down to his heart to steal a microscopic piece of the muscle for the pathologists to inspect. Finally, there was a diagnosis. It wasn't a virus at all. It wasn't something that would pass. Sam's immune system had decided to attack itself, and none of the pills he kept in the box his mother had bought for him, not the high-dose steroids his doctors prescribed nor the host of other meds—each with its own side effects that he tolerated wordlessly, belly pain and numbness and infections—could stop it.

His heart grew so sick that instead of working in sync to pump blood through his body, the chambers started to move in a dangerous rhythm called ventricular tachycardia. The doctors gave him improbably high doses of medications to calm this storm inside him, and when that did not help either, they implanted a machine under his skin, called a cardioverter defibrillator, so that when his heart slipped into this potentially lethal rhythm, a jolt of electricity would shock it back into its normal pattern. The first time it happened, it felt as if a bomb had gone off. Now the shocks were coming more and more frequently, and so he had been sent from the hospital near his home to our medical center in the hope that our team of experts could take care of him. He had been shocked by his defibrillator three times since he had arrived the night before—he might have died, that is, three times before being brought back with jolts of electricity. And we were to keep him alive while he waited for a heart transplant.

My father is a cardiologist, and when I was growing up, I liked to play with his model of the heart. It was heavy and intricate, and each of the heart's four chambers opened with a silver latch that allowed me to look inside. My father taught me the name of each part. I learned how blood travels from the body to the right atrium, through a valve to the right ventricle below it, and then out to the lungs to pick up oxygen before returning to the left side, where the pattern continues again—atrium, ventricle, out to the body. Years later, in medical school, when we cut open a cadaver and lifted the heart from its silent cage, it was beautiful and unreal. But that morning, standing outside Sam Newman's room, it was clear to me that there would be no poetry or metaphor. There was only this.

As my co-residents pored over our twenty-eight-year-old patient's electrocardiogram, jockeying to see who could name the most arcane of abnormalities in the simple tracing of his heart's rhythm, I glanced around the half-drawn curtain into the young man's room. I watched our patient lean over and pull out a laptop from the drawer next to his bed. I felt my own heart pounding, regular and insistent. Three times overnight this young man could have died, and yet there he was, alive and trying to navigate the hospital's wireless network to get on the Internet.

Sam Newman was hands down the most interesting patient in the ICU. "A great learning case," my attending pronounced that first morning. Sam was young and had a particularly nasty form of a rare disease, so I should have fought for the opportunity to be involved in even the most banal aspects of his day-to-day care. But this young man scared me. And so I avoided him. It was easy to do, at first. When we split up the daily Scut List tasks, I simply claimed the blood draws and transports and phone calls for the other patients. But one day my resident told me that the intravenous line in Sam's neck needed to come out. He had started to spike fevers, we didn't know where they were coming from, and since the catheter could represent the entry point for bacteria, one of us had to pull it. I was the intern in charge of procedures that day, so the job was mine. I put it off all morning and through our lunch of tuna fish and chicken salad sandwiches, hoping that the fevers would subside or the empty "Pull Line" box on the list would somehow disappear. But by 1 p.m., that box was still empty. "I'm going to go pull the line now," I announced to no one in particular. I grabbed one of the pale yellow gowns we wear over our clothes to keep us from transferring antibiotic-resistant bacteria from patient to patient, and stepped into his room.

I had seen him on rounds each morning, but those exams were brief, and he was often half asleep. Now, for the first time, I took in my patient. His face was swollen and his arms were bruised from the steroids that had done nothing to stop his heart's self-destruction. He was wearing a hospital gown and compression devices on his legs to prevent blood clots. Hopeful get-well cards bearing inspirational Hallmark-style messages covered the bedside table.

"Hey," I said. "I'm Daniela, one of the interns. I've seen you on morning rounds, but you've generally been sleeping."

He was typing on his laptop and barely looked up from the screen. I told him that we needed to take out his central line because it might be the source of his fevers. He shrugged, which I took as assent.

"So, here's what I'm going to do," I explained. "I'm just going to cut out the stitches. That might hurt a little. And then I'll pull out the line and hold pressure on your neck until it stops bleeding." He might bleed for a while—the fluid that his heart couldn't pump had settled in his liver, and as a result, his body wasn't working well to make his blood clot. I didn't tell him this. Instead, I told him that I was going to ask him to help me out by doing something.

"When I pull, I'm going to ask you to hum," I said.

He looked up from his computer. "Hum?" It was the first time I'd heard his voice. He sounded so regular that I felt my heart break a little. I explained that by humming, he would increase the pressure in his chest. This would decrease the chance that in the moment I pulled out the intravenous line, before I covered the tiny hole it would leave with a piece of gauze, an air bubble might enter his body, travel to his heart, and kill him before his disease would.

"Okay," he said. "Hum." He looked amused. We had asked so much of him, and this must have seemed silly in contrast. He closed his laptop and set it down on the bedside table. "I can do that."

I leaned over and gently peeled off the dressing that covered the spot where the line entered his neck. I used tiny forceps to lift the stitches and then cut them, one by one.

I had to lean in so close that I could hear him breathing. He smelled warm and a little bit like sweat, but not bad. It was time to take out the line. I lowered the head of his bed. "You all right with that?" I asked. "Uh-huh," he said.

"One, two, three. Okay now! Start humming."

"Mmmmmmmm…"

I yanked out the line and covered the spot with gauze. A drop of blood dripped down his neck, and I watched it land on his hospital gown. I moved the bed back into an upright position, my hand still on his neck. "Just a minute or two," I told him.

It was snowing outside. It was going to be a bad winter. Inside, it was quiet. "Looks like Siberia," I said to fill the silence, gesturing out the window, where snow had already blanketed the New York City streets.

My patient turned toward me, into the pressure I held on his neck, and flinched. "Sorry," I said. "Just a little longer."

He turned back. "You know, I was in Siberia once," he said.

"Really?"

I continued to hold the gauze. It was the longest I had spent in a patient's room in weeks or months, or maybe ever. He told me that he and some buddies had taken the Trans-Siberian Railway a few years back. They'd traveled all over, to places I had never seen, some I had never even heard of. "That must have been amazing," I said. It was, he told me. It was awesome. "That would be so cool to see," I offered.

"Are you on Facebook?" he asked. "I posted the photos. I'll friend you. Then you can check them out."

I lifted the piece of gauze. He had stopped bleeding. I covered the wound with fresh gauze and a piece of tape, and dropped the large IV that had been inside him into the orange biohazard bin on the other side of the room. I would let his nurse know that I had soiled his gown. "Yeah, I'm on Facebook," I said. "Line's out. I'll go tell your nurse."

Outside the room, I took a deep breath. I was sweating. I placed a big X in the empty box on the Scut List.

"That went all right?" my resident asked. "Of course," I said. Pulling out a line was barely even a procedure. "Totally fine. What's up next?"

When I got home that night, I logged on to Facebook to find a request from my patient waiting for me. I paused for a moment, then selected Accept and clicked on his name. The patient whose line I had pulled earlier that day was puffy from fluid and steroids, with a protruding belly and bruised arms and legs, but this boy on Facebook was healthy and good-looking in a way that made me think of basketball and beer. He was "single," the page said, and he liked Radiohead and Tom Clancy. He had been sending updates from the ICU. You'd have thought he was in the hospital with a sprained ankle, the way he joked, but I had held pressure on his neck that day and I knew the truth.

I didn't enter his room the next day, nor did I tell any of my co-interns about his friend request. I almost did, but then thought better of it. It would have felt, in a way, like betraying a confidence. A week passed. On rounds, we talked about how his fevers stopped and then returned. It hadn't been the line after all. Shortly afterward, my time in the cardiac ICU came to a close. I moved on to the general cardiology inpatient service, the next in my seemingly infinite intern-year lineup of rotations. My days were full. I didn't often think of our exchange. But sometimes at night, when I had opened up my computer to log on to Facebook, I found myself flipping through my patient's photos or reading his status updates. They were unfailingly optimistic. When a severe skin infection on one of his legs sent him to the operating room, he reported, "Back from surgery and doing GRRRRRREAT." Meanwhile, from his medical record, I learned that his fevers had continued, that his defibrillator kept going off, that he was still waiting for a transplant that might never come. Then one day, at least a month later, I found a message waiting for me in my Facebook inbox. It was from him. He had written, "Can I stop humming yet?"

There's a version of this story in which I replied, something friendly but restrained, and the next day I went back to the ICU to visit my patient. Maybe I would have sat down this time, and we would have talked some more about the places he'd seen while traveling and what his life was like before and what he was hoping things would be like afterward, if he got the transplant, if he did not die. Perhaps if I had done this, he could have taught me a little bit about what it is to be twenty-eight and in limbo, waiting for a transplant, for an infection, even for a re-sponse to a Facebook message. Or maybe it would have been smaller than that, and I would have done nothing more than allay a bit of his boredom before heading to noon conference. But this isn't what happened. I started to type a reply and then I stopped. I'm not sure why. Maybe I knew that I had crossed some invisible barrier. Maybe I just didn't want those boxes on the Scut List to expand into something real. I know that it wouldn't have mattered to me if he had looked at my photos or if he saw me with my friends, wearing something silly or drinking champagne out of the bottle on the way out for a night. It wasn't that. I think I was more uncomfortable with my level of investment, with how well I knew his pictures and his updates. So I signed off. I stopped looking at his page, too, scared that he would somehow sense my online footprints.

Months passed. I didn't think of him until one evening in the spring when, on a whim, I returned to his Facebook page. The pictures and status updates I knew by heart had been replaced by dozens of messages of condolence. They stretched for pages, and I read each one. Then, know-ing what I would find, I logged on to our online medical records system. After my rotation in the ICU had ended, my patient's heart rhythm had calmed and he had made it, briefly, to the general medical floor. But then his heart failure had worsened. His kidneys had shut down and he was started on dialysis. Ultimately, when it became clear that he was too sick to undergo a transplant but that he would die without one, his parents and his doctors had said, *Enough*.

He was dead. But his message was still in my inbox, hopeful and waiting. I scrolled through his profile one more time, uncertain how long a Facebook page lingers after its owner dies, before closing my computer and going to sleep.

Spring turned to summer, and by the time I became a second-year resident in charge of my own interns, I'd grown accustomed to the pace of hospital life. I worked to distill my patients into a sequence of empty Scut List boxes, as I had so rigorously been trained to do. I taught my interns to arrange CT scans and update grief-stricken families, to draw blood from the tiny veins on thumbs and feet, and to wait on hold for minutes that felt like hours to secure insurance approval for outpatient antibiotics. I fancied myself a sort of air traffic controller, the model of efficiency as I fielded phone calls and tracked lab values. If I thought at all about our overall goal, it was only to say that we were to keep our patients alive until they were discharged or someone told us not to. Goodbyes were the hasty summaries we wrote when our patients left us for the general medical floor or the brief death notes when our shocks and chest compressions had gone nowhere. There wasn't time for contemplation. There was barely even time to get the room cleaned before the next patient arrived.

I thought of that unanswered Facebook message from

time to time during my predawn treadmill sprints and in the murky moments between sleeping and waking. I even told the story to a few friends with careers outside medicine, with the same "Isn't the hospital weird?" tone I used to describe how one step of declaring death actually requires us to stick a piece of gauze in a person's eye to make sure he doesn't blink. But something about our exchange and my silence continued to bother me. And so one night, after another long day in the hospital, I decided that I would write about it. I changed my patient's name and his disease, but everything else was true. I wrote the piece in a single evening, and I couldn't have been more surprised and proud when it ran in the *New York Times* Lives section in the spring of my second year of residency. I received a message a few days later asking me to set up an appointment with one of the hospital administrators.

On the day of the meeting, I wore scrubs. I was on call and I didn't want to have to change, or else I think I would have made the effort to wear real clothes. This was the first time I had set foot in the executive suites at my hospital. I walked slowly through the wood-paneled halls, marveling at how clean and quiet it was compared to the smells and the incessant beeping and movement just a few floors up.

A trim assistant in a neat ensemble led me through the maze and ushered me into the administrator's office. I sat down in the chair across from the big wooden desk. Until that moment, I hadn't focused on why I was there and what might happen. It was only while sitting there, conspicuously underdressed and suddenly cold in my scrubs, that I realized how nervous I was. I could tolerate being disciplined for accepting my patient's friend request, if that was going to happen. I had already faced more than my share of negative responses to my piece. There were those who found me an objectionable human for my inability to reply to that Facebook message, and a terrible doctor. Some suggested I leave medicine, or if I refused to find a more suitable career path, then at least I should pursue a specialty like pathology that required minimal patient contact. That didn't hurt me. But what I couldn't stand—and the thought I found myself, all of a sudden, unable to shake— was the possibility that my patient's family was upset with me. Maybe it was wrong for me to have taken the moment that I shared with their son and told it as my own story. My stomach started to ache. There was a mini jellybean dispenser on the desk, and I turned the handle and watched as half a dozen jellybeans cascaded into my palm. I glanced at my watch. How long was this going to take?

The administrator came in a moment later. I think of him now as a tall man in a stereotypically sleek suit. We made small talk about the second year of residency and the beauty of those early summer days in the city before the air grows humid and still. I ate a couple of the jellybeans, sticky now in my hand. Then the hospital administrator told me he wanted to talk about my piece. First there was the whole Facebook thing. The hospital would now have to think about a policy regarding patient and doctor Facebook friendship. And not only had I followed my patient on Facebook; I had then looked at his online medical record—accessed his protected health information, that is—when I was no longer taking care of him. That would be understandable if it were for clinical care or for research, and even then only with the appropriate approvals, of course, but my actions seemed to have been driven more by curiosity than by anything else. That didn't deserve formal censure, he told me, but it had raised some eyebrows. Ultimately, he hoped that if and when I wrote again—and he hoped I'd continue to write (I nodded appreciatively)—I would clear the content with him beforehand. I kept nodding.

What he said was true. I had accepted a friend request, and I had indeed followed my patient's course from the intensive care unit to the general medical floor and back to the unit again, all through his online notes in the electronic medical record. I had wanted to know what had happened to him. I hadn't questioned that drive at the time, but sitting in the executive suite that day, I started to feel uncomfortable. It was curiosity plain and simple, and maybe that curiosity had crossed a line. Perhaps when my ICU rotation ended and my patient was no longer my responsibility, that's when my interest should have ended as well.

Back in medical school, I took a course in what's called "narrative medicine." The premise is that understanding the very human arc of our patients' personal histories helps us to become better doctors. We went on a field trip to the

Metropolitan Museum to look at the artwork, and we stood in front of pieces like *The Death of Socrates* and an ancient marble statue of a wounded warrior, in the hope that exposure to creative renderings of suffering might deepen our understanding of the human experience of illness. I liked the idea. I had worked as a health reporter before medical school. A good reporter tells stories, and so I thought it was natural that I would weave an understanding of my patients' narratives into the care that I delivered. As we wandered through the Met, I thought of myself in a vague fashion, as if in some kind of impressionist painting, accompanying my patients through illness as a guide and a friend. But after the tour through the museum, we didn't think about art or suffering. Instead, we went to a nearby bar and downed shots and played beer pong.

The next day, fuzzy and bleary-eyed in the lecture hall, we laughingly blamed narrative medicine for our hangovers. But still, I quietly wondered if there was something to it all. Maybe I didn't need to contemplate the art at the Met to do so, but I wanted to grow into the kind of doctor who recognizes her patients' humanity and responds with a little of her own. This version of me would always ask questions that probed each patient's fears and individual goals. I would never perform a procedure, no matter how minor, or prescribe a medication without explaining its purpose. I would never hold down a patient's arm, leaning in with all my weight, to draw blood. I would never walk in on a patient while she was on the commode and apologize but then proceed to listen to her lungs while she sat there. I would never say that I would return in the afternoon to answer questions and then not come back until the next day.

But that wasn't how it happened. I have done all of these things, not just once. It seemed that my job as a doctor in training was to accomplish the task at hand quickly and quietly, and without disrupting the flow of the work by asking too many questions. To do that successfully, I needed to grow accustomed to a system that prized efficiency, often at the expense of following my patients' stories. When I moved from the classroom onto the medical wards, I had learned that the social history—asking where the patient lived, with whom, did he own a dog, did she do drugs, what did he do for work—was fun to talk about, sure, but it was ultimately unnecessary. By the middle of intern year, I'd started to cut and paste the social history from a patient's prior notes whenever I was rushed or tired, which was most of the time, sometimes without even reading the words. It felt burdensome to ask the same questions over and over again. Moreover, the answers barely seemed to matter, since my role reached its natural end when my patients left the ICU or the hospital or the doors of my outpatient clinic.

And there in that administrative office, I was being chastised, first for crossing a line with that friend request and then for wanting to know what had happened to my patient afterward. I apologized, suddenly ashamed of a curiosity that seemed dirty. That was all I needed to hear. I didn't have to look at my patients' records once I was no longer responsible for their care. I had little time to do so anyway. There was always so much to get done. Just then my pager started to beep, a shrill and insistent sound that called me back from my contemplation, into the present. "I'm really sorry," I said, gesturing at my pager by way of explanation. "I have to go." There was a sick new admission waiting for me in the Emergency Department. I slung my stethoscope around my neck, gathered my papers, and didn't look back.

2

Ten Percent

One Saturday, a few months into the critical care sub-specialty training that had taken me from New York City to Boston, I signed up to moonlight in the Respiratory Acute Care Unit, which we refer to as the RACU, at Massachusetts General Hospital. There, I would be paid eighty dollars an hour to take care of patients who had survived an intensive care unit stay but hadn't recovered. These patients typically can't breathe without a ventilator. They are prone to infection and are often delirious, slipping from agitation to stupor. Too "stable" to require the moment-to-moment monitoring of the ICU but too sick for a general medical floor or a nursing home, these patients end up in a separate unit in the hospital, the RACU, where they remain for weeks to months. I thought of this place as purgatory. But I had a free weekend, and on a fellowship salary I'd learned not to look askance at a moonlighting shift, particularly one that would reward me with extra money for work done during the day instead of overnight.

There were ten patients on my list. One of them,

George O'Brien, was a seventy-five-year-old who hadn't left the hospital in nearly a year. He had initially come into the ICU with a severe infection that had caused his blood pressure to drop so low that his kidneys failed. Recurrent pneumonia from resistant bugs that lived in the hospital had devastated his lungs and sapped the strength he needed to be able to breathe on his own. According to the notes I read before my shift, there had been a single day about two months before when he'd actually been ready to leave the hospital. Some benign issue had postponed his discharge that day, and the rehab facility agreed to hold his bed for twenty-four hours. But the next day there was another blip—his kidney function had worsened or his blood counts had dropped—and so once again, he stayed in his hospital room. Then, it appeared to me in retrospect, the window of possibility had closed. More than three hundred days had gone by, and Mr. O'Brien had never left. It seemed he never would.

Once I finished my background reading, almost a year of life compressed into a few paragraphs and a list of infections and antibiotics, I jotted down Mr. O'Brien's overnight vital signs and approached his room to begin my morning rounds. A sign on the door announced that he was on "contact isolation" because he was having diarrhea that might have been due to *clostridium difficile,* a particularly contagious infection that can run rampant in hospitals and nursing homes. I pulled a yellow contact isolation gown over my weekend garb of scrub pants, Converse sneakers, and fleece jacket, and grabbed a pair of purple gloves. Prepped, I entered the room. Mr. O'Brien was lying on the bed, so still that at first I couldn't tell if he was even alive. He had a person's form, with its component parts of arms and legs and body and face, but he looked depleted, as if drained of some essential vitality. His eyes were half closed. His chest rose and fell with the ventilator. His legs were swollen, and yellow fluid trickled like tears from small blisters on his shins. The room smelled of talcum powder and antiseptic and bodily fluid.

When I leaned over the bed and laid the cold stethoscope on his chest, Mr. O'Brien didn't move. It was only then, as I stood over him, that I registered his wife, who was sitting silently on a chair in the corner of the room. Of course she was there, I thought. I had been told that she had been living in the hospital for the past three hundred days, too. She was a tall, thin woman whose skin and hair and clothes seemed to have faded to the same dull shade as the walls of the room. She watched, wordless, as I examined her husband. "Good morning, Mr. O'Brien," I said loudly with exaggerated cheer. He didn't react to my voice. "Mr. O'Brien?" I rubbed his shoulder. There was still no response. Months of critical illness and a few small strokes had left him in a stupor. When I moved his arm, he grimaced. ("Grimaces to pain," I would write in my daily note.)

I startled when I heard his wife's voice. "What are his

blood counts today, Doctor?" She spoke in a clipped tone. I wondered if I should make small talk, ask her about the lives she and her husband had lived before they had ended up in this room, but I was only there for the day, and she didn't seem in the mood for conversation. Thankfully, I'd already scanned through her husband's labs, so I had enough information to reply, if not to satisfy her.

"That is lower than yesterday," she said, picking up a pen and a little composition book in which she must have been writing down her husband's daily lab values. Something about her words surprised me and left me feeling, oddly, guilty. I touched her husband's legs, pushing the tip of my finger into his shin to test the depth of his swelling. The fluid gave way, and when I removed my hand, my finger left a dent. His wife was watching me. "Does he need a blood transfusion, Doctor?" He did not; his blood counts were indeed lower—likely due in some small part to our daily rituals of drawing blood to check said counts—but not yet low enough to require a transfusion. "And his kidney function today, Doctor?" It was poor. His body was still able to make urine on its own but not well enough to rid him of the excess fluid in his stomach and lungs and legs. I could still see the shadow of my fingerprint on his shin. "No change since yesterday," I told her. "Good," she replied, seemingly relieved. It wasn't good news, though, not really.

I looked at her husband for a moment, wondered if he hurt and hoped he did not, before wishing him a loud goodbye, tugging off my gown, dropping it in a bin along with my gloves, washing my hands, and leaving the room. It was time to move on to the next patient, a seventy-year-old woman with emphysema who hadn't been able to breathe on her own since an open-heart surgery. Unlike Mr. O'Brien, who was too sick to respond, she was awake, but like him, she, too, was connected to the ventilator via a surgically placed hole in her neck called a tracheostomy. As a result, she was unable to speak, and as soon as I walked into the room she started mouthing furiously.

"Hi. I'm Daniela. I'm the doctor on for the day," I introduced myself, straining to make meaning out of her moving lips. "Okay. Try to talk slowly. Are you in pain?" I asked. She shook her head, an emphatic no. I leaned in toward her, thinking maybe I would be able to hear the words in her breath. "Do you want your nurse?" Her mouth kept moving unintelligibly. "I'm sorry. One more time?" Again, she opened her mouth. She looked like she was screaming, but the air passed through the tracheostomy and into the ventilator tubing, bypassing her vocal cords and rendering her voiceless. Lipreading would be easier if she had her dentures in, but her mouth had shrunk such that they didn't fit any longer. "Maybe you can write?" She nodded. Okay, I thought. This might work. I passed her a piece of paper, a pen, and a tissue box to lean on while she wrote, but her hands were so weak that she could only make faint and ultimately undecipherable lines. When the pen slipped out of her hand and rolled under the bed, I tried to give it back but she shook her head. I had actually made her more frustrated, I still didn't know what she was trying to say, and everything was taking far longer than I intended. I leaned in again. This time I saw her lips move in a familiar motion. "You said, 'I want'!" I announced, suddenly triumphant. She nodded. "What do you want?" I watched the lips close and purse to make the *W* sound again. Two syllables. "Water? Do you want water?" She nodded. Yes! She wanted water. I scanned the information on my patient list. Of course she couldn't have water. She was weak and could easily aspirate, allowing the water to slip into her lungs. Her eyes hadn't left my face. She was getting fluids through a vein, so she was not dehydrated, but she must have missed the taste of a cold drink. I braced myself to disappoint. "You can't drink water. It's not safe," I said, as gently as I could. "I could have your nurse swab your mouth." No. That wasn't what she wanted. "I'm really sorry," I said, the same empty words that must have been offered tens of times already. I saw her eyes tear up and wanted to look away. I examined her then, stethoscope over heart and lungs, hands on belly and legs. She watched wordlessly, with her eyes fixed on me, until I left the room.

As I rubbed my hands with Purell in the hallway, one of the nurses walked by. She was a motherly woman somewhere past middle age in pink scrub bottoms and a matching pink flowered scrub top. I had heard her earlier that morning talking to some of her patients, and even to those who were too delirious to respond, people she could have just turned and washed without a word, she explained what she was doing, gently and respectfully. She touched me on the shoulder. "You're with us today in this crazy place, baby?" she said with a smile. "Sure am," I replied, looking at my watch. Two hours had passed already. But who was counting? "For the next ten hours, anyway." She was holding a few large pills and a plastic bag of the thick whitish slurry that took the place of meals for the patients who received their nutrition through feeding tubes. "There's a feast in the back room. Go help yourself, and don't miss the coffee cake! That's my recipe." I love coffee cake, particularly when I am working, stressed, or tired. I walked to the small back room at the end of the hall, which smelled deliciously like butter. She wasn't kidding. It was quite a spread. Suddenly ravenous, I cut myself a generous piece of coffee cake and ate it in a few bites. I poured a glass of orange juice to wash it down, savoring the cold liquid before I returned to the next patient on my rounding list.

Time passed slowly. On the weekend, as a moonlighter without any long-term knowledge of, or responsibility for, the patients or families, I had to maintain the status quo. We move delicately, as if afraid that if we jostle the fragile equilibrium, it'll all come crashing down, and 7 p.m. will come and go and we'll never get home. The patients are desperately ill, but most of the time they are not in any imminent danger. This is a strange feeling, disconcerting and at the same time somewhat dull.

In many ways, that dichotomy embodies chronic critical

illness. The seemingly oxymoronic phrase was coined in the 1980s to refer to patients like Mr. O'Brien, who have lived through an acute critical illness like sepsis, stroke, or trauma, but who have not yet recovered and perhaps never will. There are about one hundred thousand such people navigating this limbo of protracted sickness at any one time. Chronic critical illness is defined first by the inability to breathe without the aid of a ventilator and the resultant need for a tracheostomy tube, which offers a more stable, longer-term connection to the breathing machine. But these patients also suffer from a range of related problems—they have impaired immune systems that predispose them to infection after infection, and they are profoundly weak and delirious. Kidneys fail. Skin breaks down, leading to ulcers. In essence, nothing is working as it once did. Half of these people will die within a year. Only around one in ten will ever make it home in a state in which they are able to live independently.

Chronic critical illness isn't something we like to talk about. This shouldn't be surprising. I was drawn to critical care medicine because of its amazing technology and my desire to be part of something lifesaving, not because I wanted to know what it looked like afterward, when our interventions had successfully averted death but not in the way we had hoped. Chronic critical illness, as the name suggests, is all lingering and suffering. And so even though I had taken care of many ICU patients who would end up in this borderland, in both my residency and my fellowship, and had even been an integral part of the decisions that led to those outcomes, chronic critical illness as a result of intensive care wasn't something I had thought much about when I decided to become an ICU doctor. In fact, I hadn't even heard the term "chronic critical illness" until partway through my fellowship. I certainly hadn't ever discussed its manifestations and prognostic implications with families.

About a month before that Saturday shift, I had cared for an elderly man who had been admitted to the hospital with the flu, which had sparked an acute worsening of his emphysema. His lung disease was so severe that we had to dose him aggressively with intravenous steroids and sedate him deeply just to allow the ventilator to do its job. It was hard to imagine how he might survive. And yet, after nearly two weeks, he'd gotten better. We were decreasing the doses of his steroids. He was waking up. But he was so weak that he could barely raise his arms off the bed, and he didn't have the muscle strength to breathe on his own. And so it was time to talk about a way to connect him more permanently to the ventilator, with a tracheostomy tube.

This is a relatively minor surgery, so minor that for some patients it can be done at the bedside rather than in the OR, but it is meaningful in that it often marks the transition from acute to chronic critical illness. Like chronic critical illness itself, this isn't something we talk about. Take any one of a dozen scenes from any one of a dozen television medical shows. Doctors rush a man on a gurney into the ER. He is barely breathing. The music swells.

"We're going to need to intubate!" someone yells. Equipment appears as if by magic. A doctor takes her position at the head of the bed. Someone grabs the patient's chin and thrusts it up so that his neck is flexed. The doctor places a curved piece of metal called a laryngoscope into the patient's mouth and sweeps the tongue to the side until finally she sees the telltale V-shaped white bands that form the vocal cords. Someone passes her the plastic endotracheal tube. She advances it. The tube is in. The music slows. Disaster is averted. Cut to the next scene. After a commercial break, the patient will be ready to breathe on his own once again.

In reality, the vast majority of those who require the ventilator, say for a pneumonia or severe flare of emphysema, do indeed get better quickly enough to breathe on their own after a few days, at which point we remove the tube. But for some, this isn't the case. Days pass, and still they remain unable to breathe without the machine. Breathing tubes placed through the mouth aren't designed for long-term use. They're intrusive, and patients often require high quantities of painkillers and sedatives to tolerate the discomfort they cause. Moreover, if left in place for weeks, a breathing tube can damage the vocal cords. This is why, when we come up against the two-week mark, we begin to discuss tracheotomy. Patients with a tracheostomy tube might ultimately get strong enough to breathe and eat on their own, but not at first. So the tracheotomy is often accompanied by another procedure done on the same day by the same surgeons, which is the creation of a hole in the stomach to fit a feeding tube called a percutaneous endoscopic gastrostomy tube, or "peg." We say the words together so often they're referred to in one breath—"trach-n-peg"—or, as I've more recently heard, consolidated to a single syllable: "treg."

These procedures could represent a key decision-making moment, a pause to consider what someone might be willing to go through in order to gain more time and what sort of life a patient might consider acceptable, but in my experience, we rarely acknowledge it as such. In this recent case, as in so many others, I met with my patient's wife and their son in a small, windowless conference room outside the ICU and laid out the situation.

"Do we have a choice?" his wife asked. She wanted to tell me a little bit about her husband. He was active in his temple community. He was eighty, but that man was the life of the party, the kind of guy who danced on the tables.

I told her there was a choice. We could take him off the ventilator.

"Won't he die?" she asked me.

"Maybe," I told her. I thought of how weak he was, how even with brief trials off the ventilator his breaths grew rapid and shallow. "We would make sure that he is comfortable."

"And if we choose this surgery, will the tube ever come out?"

"We hope so. That's our goal," I said. "But we don't know."

Perhaps that's where I could have done things differently. Judith Nelson, a critical care and palliative care doctor and researcher in New York City, tends to use the words "chronic critical illness" when she is talking to families about these decisions, and she tells them it has a prognosis worse than some cancers. Few have ever heard this term, so she gives them the language to think beyond the individual procedures and turn this nebulous state into a diagnosis. It's not that she wants to dissuade family members from pursuing aggressive interventions. Her goal is to explain the possibilities of what life might look like moving forward, so that the decisions people make—not just the decision surrounding trach, but also the countless choices, some smaller and some bigger, that likely follow—can be as well-informed and realistic as possible. "People are willing to play very long odds, and I do want to support that," she told me. "The question is how to at once let them get the full benefit of intensive care and all its promise and still protect them from a really bad end."

When I returned to my patient's room the next morning, his wife told me that they had made their decision. They would go ahead with the tracheotomy. There was an opening in the OR schedule, and my patient came back to the ICU with a trach and peg later that afternoon.

I found myself replaying that conversation as the hours of my weekend RACU shift ticked by, punctuated by pages and trips to the back room for one more slice of coffee cake. Last I had heard, that patient was still in the ICU, battling a new pneumonia. If he got through that infection, he, too, would probably be transferred to the Respiratory Acute Care Unit, where I might see him on another moonlighting shift. But what would come after? I wondered whether his wife had understood (if it was even possible for her to understand) what she was signing up for when she agreed to the trach. Looking around me that day, I wondered if any of the patients and families I had ushered into the worlds of trach tubes and ventilators had known that it might be like this. And if they had, would anything about their decisions have changed?

One of the difficulties of communicating about chronic critical illness is that the course doesn't always look like Mr. O'Brien's. It often does; there is a slow decline punctuated by infections, delirium, and organ failure. But there are outliers, too. For all the likelihood of turning out like Mr. O'Brien, there is also the possibility of another story, that of a man named Charlie Atkinson.

When I first met Charlie one spring afternoon, he hadn't been home for nearly nine months. In a stroke of amazingly bad luck for the social, athletic seventy-six-year-old, a bite from a mosquito at an early evening outdoor cocktail party had left Charlie with a severe case of West Nile virus. The virus nearly killed him, but after weeks in the ICU he had emerged—alive, yet unable to breathe without a ventilator. West Nile had resulted in a poliolike paralysis that meant Charlie couldn't move his arms or legs. He was delirious.

He underwent a tracheotomy and placement of a feeding tube, and was eventually transferred from the ICU to the RACU, where he spent another few weeks. At that point, by some parameters Charlie was well enough to leave the hospital. After all, his labs and blood pressure were stable. But barely able to move even a finger, tethered to the ventilator, responsive to his name but little else, Charlie couldn't go home. So from the RACU, Charlie was transferred to another kind of hospital, one specifically for patients who were still sick enough to need ventilators or tracheostomy tubes, but not so sick that they required the monitoring and nursing intensity of an intensive care unit or even the RACU. This is a hospital that families like Charlie's and many doctors, particularly doctors in training working in traditional hospitals, have never set foot in, called a "long-term acute care hospital," or LTACH.

Back in residency, when I was called upon to explain an upcoming LTACH transfer to a family member and trying to stay positive, I generally described it as "going to rehab." I suspected this gave families the hopeful and likely mistaken idea that their vent-dependent delirious loved one would end up on a treadmill, but I really wasn't certain what else went on in such a facility. Nearly a year into my fellowship training to be a critical care doctor, I still had never entered an LTACH. But I knew that if I hoped to discuss with chronically critically ill patients and their families what might be ahead, I would need to better understand what the next step looked like. So one spring day,

I made the same trip many of my patients had, from MGH to our hospital-affiliated LTACH, the Spaulding Hospital for Continuing Medical Care. I hoped to find some patients or families who were willing to tell me a bit about what their lives were like there.

I wasn't sure what to expect and was surprised to walk up to a pleasant-looking brick building off a tree-lined road in a quiet, largely residential part of Cambridge, just minutes from the youthful pulse of Harvard Square. There was an ambulance bay around the side, but the front entrance looked to me more like a nursing home than anything else. The lobby was small and disquietingly still—entirely unlike the buzzing hospital lobbies to which I had grown accustomed, with their overhead alarms and doctors reaching for their ringing pagers and the click of heels on tile floor. The elevator was ponderously slow, yet no one seemed to mind. When it finally deposited me on the third floor, where most of the patients who needed ventilators were roomed, the first thing I noticed was the sound. It was reassuringly familiar; I was in a hospital, after all. There was the jarring, intermittent beeping of the ventilator and heart rate monitors, doctors and nurses talking about their patients' lab values and how someone needs a CT scan and who is going away for the weekend and what they should get for lunch and whether ten in the morning is too early to place the food order. Stacks of yellow isolation gowns sat outside the rooms, and the halls smelled of stool and antiseptic and powder. In this way, it was like an intensive care unit. But

I felt a sort of fatigue here, too, a sense of tired resignation to an undesirable set of facts. If progress were to come, it would take weeks to months, not hours or days. Time begins to expand in the move from the intensive care unit to the RACU, and here, it seemed to have slowed even more.

I walked up and down the main hallway on the vent floor, peering into a few of the rooms only to stand, uselessly, in front of patients much like Mr. O'Brien, who weren't able to respond. I was starting to wonder if I should just leave—not only was I suddenly overwhelmed by the feeling of exhausted sadness that surrounded me, but I was frustrated by my inability to find someone who might be able to talk—when one of the Spaulding doctors directed me to Charlie Atkinson's room. I peered in. Even diminished by the hospital bed, Charlie was clearly a tall man, with a thick head of gray hair and distinguished, patrician features. And he was awake and alert, his eyes bright. "Come in," he beckoned as I paused in the doorway. That April morning, he wore a hospital gown, compression stockings, and an insulated glove on one of his hands. West Nile virus had left him with nerve damage, and he'd found that keeping the hand warm was the one way to diminish the shooting pains. Although he was breathing on his own through his tracheostomy tube during the day, he still needed the ventilator overnight. Behind his bed were the usual suction catheters, wall hookups for oxygen, and IV poles. A collage on the windowsill showed pictures of a debonair gentleman with his college friends at Harvard reunion events and smiling with his family.

As I stood by Charlie's bed to introduce myself, he started to cough. It was a deep, throaty sound, somewhat jarring even for the ears of a doctor in the midst of critical care training. His eyes began to tear as he worked to bring up the phlegm and cough it out through his tracheostomy tube. I felt a twinge of discomfort myself, and was looking toward the suctioning equipment behind his bed when his wife, Jeannette, a slight woman who moved quickly with a competent air, walked in. Without skipping a beat, she pulled on a pair of gloves, slipped the cap off her husband's trach tube, took the suction catheter from the wall, and fed it down Charlie's trachea. He coughed and gagged, face turning red, then purple. Seemingly unshaken, Jeannette withdrew the suction catheter and with it the grayish culprit plug of mucus. She capped the tube. Charlie stopped coughing. Husband and wife turned and looked toward me, and I repeated my introduction to Jeannette while she removed her gloves. "Do you want to go down the hall to talk?" she asked. "That sounds great," I replied. I would return to talk with Charlie later.

Jeannette and I walked out of the room and down to a few chairs set up at the end of the hall. From the window, I could see the parking lot. The snow had finally melted and the trees were starting to bud. When Charlie had been transferred to Spaulding from MGH, his wife told me, she'd had little idea of what lay ahead. She was simply relieved that he had survived. "The intensive care doctors were pleased that he's alive and he's going to rehab, and isn't that great. I felt pleased, too," she said. But when he got to Spaulding, Charlie was still delirious and so weak that he could barely move. He still needed the ventilator off and on. No one mentioned the term "chronic critical illness," but a few months into his Spaulding stay, Jeannette was told that Charlie had reached a plateau, and his doctors at the LTACH started to encourage her to look at nursing homes, which we call skilled nursing facilities (or SNF, pronounced *sniff*). I had asked one of the doctors at Spaulding what happens when patients don't get better. "They end up going to SNFs, most of them," he had told me. "Or they die."

That winter, Jeannette drove to facilities some sixty miles from her home in Cambridge, and as she walked through each of them she wondered whether she could imagine her husband there. The options were scant. Though Charlie was off the vent by then, he was still delirious, he had the trach, and he needed a machine to help his weak muscles even muster up a cough, which meant that he was a more medically complex patient than most nursing homes would handle. So Jeannette tried to figure out if she could bring her husband home—theoretically she could, she remembered being told, but the costs of the care he needed at that point would have totaled more than half a million yearly. "That was the most awful month," Jeannette remembered. But then, slowly, things started to shift.

50

First, one of Charlie's doctors decided that he should go back on the ventilator regularly at night. That might have seemed like a step backward, but with the extra respiratory muscle rest, Charlie's strength started to improve. His continued need for the ventilator meant he still required the monitoring that the long-term acute care hospital offered, so the looming threat of the nursing home was at least temporarily diminished. And with the aid of a particularly tough and dedicated physical therapist's "boot camp," Charlie began to move. By the time I met him, that spring, he still could not walk, but after an excruciating ceiling lift transfer from his bed to his wheelchair, his physical therapists could help him use his arms to hoist his body into a standing position at the parallel bars. He could sit at the edge of his bed with assistance. His mind was clearing. His family arranged for a massage therapist, a young man with a gentle demeanor, to visit him a few nights a week. They played music, Leonard Cohen sometimes or Olivia Newton-John.

And after months in what sounded to me like limbo, Charlie started to set goals, which he spoke aloud and recorded for himself on his iPhone. He was planning to go home, he told me when I returned to his room—he still needed the ventilator, but would no longer need the exorbitantly expensive twenty-four-hour trained nursing care. He had already started looking for hospital beds online. Though the trach tube had weakened his voice, his tone was confident, and I heard in it glimmers of a past life as an entrepreneur who imagined and then built new companies from the ground up. He would get home by the fall, more than a year after he had been rushed to MGH, he said. I wanted to believe him. Maybe he could beat the odds.

A few months after I met Charlie, I returned to the RACU for my official rotation. I'd be on for a month. Twelve-hour days, but at least we had weekends off. Some of my co-fellows spoke glowingly about their RACU rotations and the physiology they learned through caring for the survivors of intensive care, but I remembered my moonlighting day and the pain I perceived and my frustration. I'm not sure what it said about me, but I knew that I wouldn't be able to enjoy learning about respiratory muscle weakness when the smell of it lingered on my clothes even after I'd gone home.

I started my first day in the RACU with a run on the treadmill near my apartment. I lived just across the street from MGH, so I was able to finish showering at 6:45 and arrive at the hospital with my hair dripping wet and my face still red from my run just minutes after 7 a.m. In the fellows' lounge, I poured myself a coffee and picked up my list from the junior attending who had been on overnight. I'd gotten a rundown on the patients from my co-fellow the night before, so I scanned through the list that morning to see if anything had changed. Overnight, someone had been increasingly delirious and someone had had to go back on the vent and someone else had received intravenous fluids for low blood pressure. The names meant little to me—except for Mr. O'Brien. Months after my moonlighting shift, he was still there.

My attending was waiting for me at the desk where we sat between patient exams to review the plans for the day. He was a pale, slight, soft-spoken man with a dry sense of humor who spent all but six weeks each year in the laboratory, researching the biochemical mechanisms behind rare lung diseases. He would oversee me as we worked together to move our patients closer to some goal—although as we rounded that morning, and again the next day and the day after that, I realized that it wasn't clear to me what that goal was, let alone how to get there.

I fell into a tolerable pattern. In the morning, I ran on the treadmill fast and hard, powered by the most invigorating music I could find. Then a coffee gulped down in the fellows' lounge, then rounds, lunch, maybe a bronchoscopy to suck out tenacious secretions, a trach change, a few blood draws or consults called, and soon enough it was 7 p.m. and time to sign out again. The rotation continued this way until late one afternoon, when a nurse called over to the desk where I was sitting in front of the computer to order the next day's labs. "Can someone come to room 28?"

Her tone sounded urgent. Room 28…I could never understand why the nurses tended to use room numbers instead of names. I looked down at my list: that was Mr. O'Brien's room. My attending had already left for the day. I grabbed my papers and walked over quickly, pulling on a yellow isolation gown, squirting some Purell into my hands, and grabbing a pair of gloves before stepping in. To my surprise, he didn't look any different than usual. It was only the monitor above his bed that revealed a change and the reason for the nurse's concern: Mr. O'Brien had a fever, his heart rate was high and blood pressure precariously low.

Each day on rounds that week, I had wondered if we should start with Mr. O'Brien or save him till last. I felt I was never able to answer his wife's questions fully. With her continued fixation on her husband's renal function and her entirely unrealistic certainty that he would one day come home again, she made me feel nervous and somewhat defensive. Although her husband appeared much the same as he had on my moonlighting shift those many months earlier—which is to say, dreadfully ill but alive— his kidney function had been slowly worsening. On one hand, I'd started to think of him as possibly immortal, but on the other, I knew that it was just a matter of time until another bleed or an infection threw off the strange equilibrium he had maintained for so many months.

That afternoon, after pausing a few beats to assess the room, I took his wife aside. I tried to explain that her husband likely had yet another infection, or maybe he was bleeding somewhere, but whatever it was, he was too weak to fight it. This might be the last in the long line of insults to his body that had brought him farther and farther from the goal of one day getting home. I wanted to tell her that he was dying, but I found that I couldn't say the words.

As I stood there, momentarily silent, I realized that despite seeing Mr. O'Brien every morning, I didn't really know anything about him. I had no idea what he had been like before he came into the hospital, whether he had a good sense of humor, what kind of work he'd done, or how he had spent his free time. I knew he had a daughter, because I had seen her visit occasionally, and I knew she brought cookies for the nurses when she came, but that was all. And his wife barely knew or had any reason to trust me—I was just the latest in a long line of doctors who had passed through this room. Now, with the monitors beeping to alert me to my patient's dangerously low blood pressure, it felt far too late to start asking anything.

His wife was looking at me. "There are medicines you can give him?" she asked, her words a mixture of a question and a statement. There were medicines. There are almost always medicines, I wanted to say, but her husband had not been able to breathe on his own or go outside or experience anything, as far as we could perceive, other than discomfort in months. Even if we could get him over this hurdle, what were we returning him to? "Yes, there are medicines. We can give him fluids and more antibiotics, and we can start meds that can raise his blood pressure," I responded. These medicines, called vasopressors, act directly on the heart and are administered through a central line, a large catheter in the internal jugular vein. Like any medical intervention, the act of starting pressors can cause harm—placement of the catheter can be painful, there is a small risk of hitting the carotid or puncturing the lung, the meds themselves can result in irregular heart rhythms. And if we are serving only to prolong a death that is inevitable... Mr. O'Brien's wife was looking at me expectantly. "We can start the meds for the blood pressure right now, but then he'll need another procedure to put a big catheter in his neck. We'll need to send him to the ICU for that." I took another breath. There was more to say. "I'm worried that even if we do all of those things, we still won't be able to make him better." His wife did not pause. "Give him the medicine," she said. His blood pressure was dropping, and fluid alone would not be enough to turn it around. So I did.

By the end of the evening, we had decided to move Mr. O'Brien to the ICU. His wife followed behind the stretcher, carrying a small bag of clothes and her notebook. They had been in the hospital for nearly a year, and I was surprised she did not have more. A few days later, I learned, Mr. O'Brien died. His wife went home. Late that night, she called the ICU and asked to speak with the doctors who'd pronounced her husband dead. She had a request.

The intern got on the phone. "Hello?" he said. On the other end of the line, Mrs. O'Brien spoke. "They say my husband died tonight, but I just... I'm not sure he's dead," she said. "Would someone check the morgue?"

From time to time during my weeks in the RACU and in

the months that followed, I thought of Charlie Atkinson. Learning what I had about the outcomes of chronic critical illness, I wondered if he had made it home. I envisioned him still in his room at Spaulding. Perhaps he had fallen prey to another infection, and I imagined him delirious once again, ventilator dependent and bedbound. When we had last talked, Charlie and his wife had given me their e-mail addresses. He had told me he hoped to get home by the fall, so that December I sent him an e-mail. I doubted that I would hear back, but after caring for Mr. O'Brien, it seemed somehow important for me to find out what had happened.

To my surprise, Charlie wrote back soon afterward. He'd made it out of Spaulding, and although he continued to struggle with infections, weakness, and painful neuropathy, he was home.

One evening the following week, I found myself in front of the Atkinson house, next to the wheelchair ramp Charlie's family had installed prior to his return. The air was chilly in early December, and at 5:30 it was already dark outside. I felt a little odd standing at Charlie's door at first, but I put aside my concerns when Jeannette greeted me warmly with a hug. She was thrilled that I could make it over for dinner, she told me, and Charlie was excited to talk with me. He was waiting in the dining room that they'd converted into a bedroom so he could spend his days on the first floor. She would take me to him.

Back at Spaulding, Charlie had told me about the hospital bed he'd ordered from eBay. He was lying on it, not in
a hospital gown this time but in a comfortable gray sweat-
shirt and shorts. A home ventilator sat next to his bed,
with the tubing to connect to the tracheostomy in his neck.
A urinary catheter snaked its way out of the pant leg of
his shorts. As we talked, he cleared his throat frequently
to bring the phlegm up through his trach. He couldn't be
alone and so had hired two live-in caregivers, a cabaret
singer and a piano player from a local music school, who
looked after him in exchange for room and board. Even so,
there had been a scare with his trach one night a few weeks
back, and a moment that he would not forget, when he
wasn't getting enough air and thought that he might die.
But the emergency had been averted, and he was safe at
home with his wife in the elegant Cambridge house where
they'd raised their children and lived for decades. I could
smell dinner cooking, and at Charlie's behest, I followed
tentatively behind him and his walker as we made our way
toward the kitchen. Jeannette had prepared a full meal of
roast chicken, asparagus, and rice. She poured me a generous glass of wine, and as we ate, warmed by the food
and the wine, the conversation turned to chronic critical
illness—the weeks, months, and even years some patients
and families spend in the hospital, hoping for a recovery
that might never come. Despite their year in this world,
neither Charlie nor Jeannette had ever heard the term
"chronic critical illness," nor had they any idea of its associ-

ated prognoses. I felt as though I was inducting them into a strange club that Charlie had unknowingly been a member of since the day he'd undergone a tracheotomy.

We finished our chicken, and while I talked, Jeannette started to clear our plates. I stood up to help but she gestured at me to sit down. I was the guest. From the oven, she brought out a freshly baked apple cobbler and carried it over to the table. I took a large piece and a scoop of vanilla ice cream. While our ice cream melted over the apples, I watched Charlie and his wife contemplate what I'd told them. It is easier, but perhaps neither fair nor fully honest, to consider chronic critical illness from this vantage point, in a family kitchen enjoying the familiar smells of chicken and apple and cinnamon. Perhaps as a result, Charlie's response to me was not that he wished someone had discussed chronic critical illness with him when he was at Spaulding. Instead, he was pleased to find that he was even luckier than he had imagined. "Did you hear that, honey?" he exclaimed, turning to his wife. "Ten percent make it home!" I probed a little bit more. I asked Charlie whether he thought knowing about these outcomes might have changed his perspective during the winter when Jeannette was looking at nursing homes and he seemed to have reached a plateau. By way of response, Charlie told me that in college he had been a rower. He paused to clear his throat, as if to give me time to consider the unique combination of personal resolve, financial reserve, immense family support, and plain luck that had allowed him to get home despite those odds, more than a year after he had left the ICU. "I know how to put the oar in one more time," he said.

After dinner, Charlie and Jeannette said goodnight to me before heading to the first floor bathroom. It was time for Jeannette to suction the secretions from her husband's tracheostomy tube before bed.

Nearly a year later, I received another e-mail from Charlie Atkinson. It was a paperless invitation. He had been home one year, and he was throwing a party to celebrate. I decided to stop by and invited a friend who, I had recently learned, was one of the doctors who'd taken care of Charlie on his first day at MGH. She and her intern had struggled to perform a spinal tap, inserting the long thin needle between Charlie's vertebrae to obtain a sample of his spinal fluid. He had been too confused and stiff to get his body into the right position for the test, which would have required him to curl his legs up to his chest in a fetal position to increase the space between the vertebrae. They tried multiple times before calling it quits. The neurologists came in next and finally succeeded, getting a sample of the fluid that would ultimately return a positive result for West Nile virus.

At the party that evening, my friend told Charlie all of this and he listened, fascinated. He hadn't heard that part of his story before, and he remembered none of it. She was intrigued, too, watching Charlie eat cheese and crackers, chatting with his son and buddies from college. After all, she had last seen him lying in that hospital bed more than two years earlier, spiking fevers, barely responsive. At that time she had imagined his likely outcome as death, or life with impairments so severe that he'd never make it home.

For my colleagues and me, the time in the hospital when we intersect with patients like Charlie or Mr. O'Brien is generally all we know of their trajectories. Perhaps we see them if they get sick enough to return to the unit and if that readmission coincides with our time on service. But we rarely have the opportunity to follow them out through long-term acute care hospitals, infections, delirium, readmissions, and maybe, if they are very lucky, back home to a life that looks something like what they left.

Charlie Atkinson and Mr. O'Brien passed through some of the same doors, but one was home and the other never made it out. When did they diverge? Perhaps there wasn't one specific point but a slow progression, moment after moment, setback after setback. In hindsight, at the Atkinson home that night, I wondered how similar they really were. Both were chronically critically ill, yes, but perhaps Charlie Atkinson had never really been as sick as Mr. O'Brien was. Despite the encephalitis and the respiratory muscle weakness that left Charlie dependent on the ventilator, his other organs—his kidneys, his heart, ultimately his brain—remained intact, while Mr. O'Brien appeared, when I met him, to have fallen apart slowly, piece by piece.

Charlie and Jeannette were in many ways exceptional; this much was clear to me. But still I wondered: at what point in the course of chronic critical illness do you know who is going to be Charlie—or maybe, who *can* be Charlie, with all the personal resources and trade-offs and simple luck that being Charlie requires—who is going to be Mr. O'Brien, and who will end up in the vast in-between? After my first dinner with the Atkinsons, I had posed this question to Judith Nelson, the New York City intensive care and palliative care doctor who conducts research on chronic critical illness. "I don't know when it becomes clear if it isn't going to be okay," she had told me. "But at some point, it does, or something develops that's unacceptable to the patient, like it's clear they're never going to go home. And so I think every day, you just keep weighing the benefits of continuing the treatments against the harms, every single day."

For someone else in Charlie's place, that calculation might well have come out differently, particularly in the winter days at Spaulding when Jeannette was looking at nursing facilities and it seemed as though he might never make it home. But there he was, in his kitchen, gesturing to his son to take out his smartphone to videotape the event. I watched as a younger version of Charlie held up the phone in video camera mode and recorded his father working the crowd. Charlie leaned on a walker and still needed a urinary catheter, but his doctors had been able to take out his tracheostomy tube, and only a small scar on his neck marked his months of intermittent ventilator dependence. He looked good. My mind wandered. I imagined an evening at Spaulding, just a few miles away, where the ventilator alarms sounded, a patient called his nurse for suctioning, and a husband sat anxiously by his wife's bedside. Then my thoughts turned to Mrs. O'Brien, and I imagined her on that same evening. Maybe she was eating dinner in the house she'd shared with her husband. After nearly a year of doctors, decisions, uncertainty, and hope, it was over. Her husband was never coming home. And she was alone.

3

Life on Battery

His heart was failing. I imagine it was like this: His legs were swollen and heavy like weights. He was so tired. But when he lay down in bed, he felt he was drowning, and so he started to sleep propped up on the couch. He had taken all the medicines his doctors prescribed him, and they each helped a little, but they did not help enough. Van Chauvin was not afraid of dying but he did not want to go on living this way, suffocating in the night.

And then his doctors told him about something else. Something called a left-ventricular assist device, nicknamed LVAD, or just VAD. They told him that the machine would work by drawing blood from a chamber of his heart and propelling it into his aorta—the main vessel that carries blood throughout the body—at a pressure high enough to keep him going far better than his failing heart could manage. A cable called a driveline would run from the device and out of his body by way of a hole the surgeons would create in his abdomen. He would have to take good care of this hole to make sure it didn't get infected. A bad infection could kill him, they said. This cable would lead to a battery-powered "controller unit" that he'd wear on his waist, strapped to an elastic belt. If this device did not incapacitate him by causing a stroke or a bleed, it might allow him to walk comfortably again. He might be able to sleep in his bed. Though some people receive the VAD as a "bridge," a way to stay alive while waiting for a heart transplant that might or might not come, Van had been a smoker his entire life, so he wasn't a candidate for a heart. He might get on the list eventually, but if he didn't, his VAD would be a "destination." That's how he would live until he died—battery-powered during the day and plugged into the wall to recharge at night.

There is something about this machine that I have found fascinating since I first learned about it in residency. During an intern year elective, I spent time working with a cardiologist who studies mechanical devices that support the failing heart. I'd thought that I would become a cardiologist like my father, and though that idea didn't stick, I remember that I was entranced by my attending's clear explanations of the inner workings of the VAD, delivered in his crisp, German-accented English. Sitting in his office on one of the top floors of Columbia University's medical research building, I held an early version of this device and passed the equipment from one hand to the other. It felt solid and sturdy, and if I had not known its purpose, I would have thought it just an unassuming piece of metal and plastic machinery.

In some ways, it's nothing more than another implantable device, much like an insulin pump for diabetics or a cochlear implant for the deaf. I know the heart is just a muscle, and I have held a cadaver's still heart in my hands and felt its inanimate weight. Even so, I can't help but believe that there's something more to it all, some kind of meaning I can't ignore in the fact that thousands of people today are staying alive by plugging themselves into a wall socket each night. This very conspicuous melding of human and machine has long struck me as a life at the edge, and this edge was one that even in the early days of my intern year I felt was important to understand. Of course, as a critical care doctor and not a surgeon, I'm never going to be the one implanting these devices. And I know that as time passes, these devices will become smaller, as devices do, the external parts will become internal, and one day the VAD might be no clumsier or more metaphorically powerful than a pacemaker. But there will always be another machine that goes one step further to bring us up against the limits of what it is to be mortal. And as a doctor who cares for people at these margins, I wanted to understand what it was like to live a life enabled by this kind of technology—not just amid the buzz of acute care decision-making, but after, when the reality set in.

Van Chauvin trundled down the shiny white hallway of the cardiology clinic offices. The hospital can feel like a maze, but Van and his sister Donna, who'd accompanied him on the drive from their home in central Massachusetts into the city, had learned it inside and out. They had been here so many times—too many—ever since Van's heart failed and his doctors implanted a VAD in his chest.

He was slightly disheveled, hustling from one waiting room to the next in the camouflage-print hunting vest he had bought at Walmart some years back. These days, instead of carrying the fishing tackle he would have preferred, each vest pocket held one of two backup batteries to power his VAD. Even so, with his camo vest, burly frame, and graying beard, the sixty-year-old looked more like an aging outdoorsman than a heart failure patient dutifully toting the equipment that kept blood pumping through his body.

When his doctors first told him about the machine, I imagine that Van wanted to know what his life would be like. Actually, that's not quite right. What I think Van Chauvin must have wanted first, what I think that I would have wanted, anyhow, was for it all just to disappear. He was in his midfifties, and before his health had gone to hell he'd been a smoker and a drinker, easily frustrated and quick to anger. His marriage had failed but he had three adult children to show for it. He'd found steady work at a warehouse making building supplies and taken up a hobby: raising birds— macaws, African gray parrots, cockatiels. At first, when his breath grew short, he didn't know it was his heart. He didn't know it was anything at all. It is amazing what you can learn to ignore. But then his head started to spin, the world went gray, and he thought he would collapse there on the hard floor of the warehouse. So he saw a doctor.

She referred him to a specialist. When the cardiologist examined him and listened to his story, she knew she had to send him for an ultrasound of his heart. He might have shivered a bit when the cold ultrasound jelly touched his chest. Maybe he wanted to ask about the grainy pictures on the screen next to him and what they meant, but instead he was quiet. Later that week, he learned that his heart was barely pumping at all. His doctors gave him medicines to take every day, in the morning and at night. He got used to the feeling of the pills in his mouth. He'd never been one for doctors or medicine, but it seemed as though they were doing the job. That was good. He swore off alcohol and joined AA. He went back to the warehouse, and he was slower than he had been but he could still get his work done. Then his doctors told him that he needed something else—a machine that would sit under the pectoralis muscle in his chest and shock him back to life with a jolt of electricity if his heart misfired or stopped pumping. He didn't think much about this. It would just be a small thing, the defibrillator. So he said yes.

It exploded inside his chest five times and maybe more. He lost count. Each time the shock rocked him, but then it was over. He would have died without the machine, but there he was, still alive. And he was feeling pretty good. He took a road trip with a friend. They drove up and down the East Coast selling leather jackets, chaps, and T-shirts at bike shows. Mardi Gras came, and even though he wasn't drinking anymore, he made it to New Orleans and had a great time. He felt so good he even started a project. He decided he was going to build a camping trailer, so he hauled off to Home Depot for plywood and plastic sheeting, and then he bought himself a flatbed to use as the base. He stored it all in a garage he shared with a friend, and in his spare time he worked on it for a few hours each day. He got winded, and there was the threat of the explosion in his chest, but he was better than he had been, back when everything started.

Van took all the medicines his doctors prescribed. He was still smoking, but he hadn't picked up a drink since his heart had given out. If he'd been the sort to think this way, he might have felt it unjust when his legs started to swell again, when he became dizzy and couldn't catch his breath. The camper parts grew dusty, unattended in the garage. He couldn't even go fishing on the lake when the weather was warm. Merely getting off the couch made his heart race, and it took all the energy in the world to stand, just to exist. So he went to the hospital and waited in the ER until they finally found him a bed. They placed an IV in his arm to give him medicines that would help him clear the fluid that had settled in his lungs and his belly and his legs because his heart couldn't pump it. This made him feel lighter and better, and he went back home thinking that maybe things would be different. But a few days later, the cycle began again. He was getting sicker, and it seemed as if nothing was able to help him. That's when his doctors started to talk about sending him to Boston for another device, a bigger one called a VAD.

With the machine, they said, the odds that he'd be alive in a year were higher than without. But that life would come with new risk and significant hardship. He could have a massive stroke or a dangerous bleed. He might have to go back to the OR for another surgery to replace the machine's pump. He wouldn't be able to take a swim or go out in a boat because the VAD can't get wet. Deciding against the machine might mean a shorter life but one that could be spent at home, with fewer appointments and admissions to the hospital. It would be his choice.

Van had actually heard of this device before, some seven years back when his brother Paul had gotten sick. Paul was much worse off than Van had ever been, and when Paul ended up in the hospital with his heart barely working, his doctors had a similar conversation with the Chauvin family. The family had said yes to the VAD right away. Paul was in the hospital for three months and he got the device, but it didn't matter because he died anyway, swollen and comatose, hooked to machines that did not save him.

So Van thought about Paul, of course. He'd seen his brother die, and his mother had seen it, too, as had his sisters, and none of them wanted to lose Van that way. But they didn't want to say no, either. After all, it had been seven years. They figured the machines must have gotten better in that time, and while Van was not a small man, he was thinner and healthier overall than his brother had been. As scared as they were, the family believed in Van's doctors, and they believed, too, in the hopeful forward march of medicine and technology. The way they saw it, this was Van's best chance. As for Van, he remembered Paul and the way he'd lain there in the hospital bed day after day. Then he thought of what his own life had become: breathlessness, drowning, a couch, the ER. That was what scared him. He figured that if he died, it would be like falling asleep and then it would be over. But if the VAD worked, it would be a "spare tire" that would let him get back to the independent life he craved. Besides, he liked his doctors and he trusted them. So if they gave him the okay, he'd go with the VAD.

One Sunday morning, I rented a car to head out to Van's home, some sixty miles southwest of Boston, near the Connecticut border. I had spent a morning observing VAD clinic on what just happened to be the day of Van's most recent appointment, and one of the doctors there suggested I might enjoy his perspective. When I told Van that I was a lung doctor interested in learning more about what it is like to live with a VAD, his face broke into an incredulous smile. He told me that if I really wanted to know about his life, I shouldn't talk with him there, between clinic appointments, when he was aggravated and distracted waiting for his name to be called. I should come see him at his home. I was happy to receive the invitation. I wanted to know how and where he plugged in, and whether the cord was able to reach the bathroom at night, and what happened when the alarm went off, and whether he was able to react without terror. I wondered how he'd been able to come to terms with the new limitations imposed by living with the VAD, and whether he ever felt misgivings about the decision to go ahead and receive the device.

I had stopped by a monthly support group for patients with VADs and their family members earlier that same week. The group met in one of the conference rooms on the main cardiac floor of the hospital. A handful of people in a mix of street clothes and inpatient gowns were already sitting on the couches when I arrived. I took a seat just in time to hear one woman lean in to the group and explain that she hadn't been sure her husband should get the VAD because she didn't know if she could act as his caregiver. She looked to be in her late sixties, neatly dressed in slacks, loafers, and a pressed button-down shirt. When her husband had first heard about the VAD, he had been all for it, she said, hopeful that the machine could extend and improve the quality of his life. But she was still working—even in the hospital, she tried to get in a few hours with her laptop each day, just to clear her mind— and as much as she loved this man, she'd struggled with the idea that she would be the one to do his dressing changes and react to the machine's alarm, day after day. She honestly didn't know if she had the stomach for it.

As she talked, my eyes moved to her husband, who was

sitting beside her. Illness had aged him, and he was quiet, dressed in a gown and slippers, hooked to an IV pole with battery packs hanging over his shoulder. He'd gone with the VAD after all and was recovering from the surgery.

She was still scared, she told us. She knew that things could go wrong. Her husband could suffer a stroke or a bleed that would leave him unmoving and unthinking, but alive thanks to the machine in his chest. What would they do then? Maybe her husband would end up with cancer, and then they would have to decide whether and when and how to turn the machine off. Maybe the machine would malfunction. Or maybe it would work just as it was supposed to for a while, but she would mess up the dressing changes and the cable's entry site would get infected. What if she froze the first time the alarm went off and forgot how to change the batteries? None of it would be easy. Yet they'd been married for nearly half a century. If everything went as well as it possibly could, the device would let her husband live longer and better, giving him back some of the energy his heart failure had sapped. He wanted that chance. And she'd taken a vow—granted, she had never envisioned becoming the caregiver of a husband kept alive by a battery-operated artificial heart, but it was a vow nonetheless. She felt she owed her husband this. So she'd gotten on board.

Driving down the long stretch of highway from Boston to Van's house, my mind wandered to that support group. I wondered what would happen to that woman and her husband, whether the VAD would give him back some of the life that he missed and whether she would be able to return to work. We'd also heard from a gregarious younger man in track pants who had gone from a VAD to a transplant a year before. He came in late and dominated the conversation once he arrived, but in a likable way that made it clear how proud he was of what he had gone through and how well he was doing. I hoped he would stay healthy. I hoped for the quiet ones, too, those who worried silently. I could imagine each of them in the hospital, me at their bedside in scrubs, monitoring labs and titrating medications and then, when they grew strong enough to stand and walk and begin to complain about the food, arranging their discharge paperwork. But that's where my imagination ended. I didn't have the faintest idea what happened next for these people and their machines, beyond the structure and safety of the hospital's architecture.

Van lived in a community for the elderly and disabled, in a complex of identical houses. I got lost trying to find his home, and so I pulled over and called his phone number. One of his sisters answered the phone. She stood out on the stoop waving excitedly as soon as she saw my car, greeted me with a hug although we had never met before, and led me inside. I stepped through the door and into the living room. When we'd talked, Van had seemed uncertain that any of his family members would have the time to drop by, and I expected it would probably just be him and maybe one of his sisters. I assumed that I would take a look at the device, we would make small talk, and then I would leave. So I did a double take as I entered the living room; it was as if I had stumbled into a holiday gathering. There was Darlene, whom I'd just met outside, and Donna, who regularly accompanied Van through the clinic labyrinth. The small elderly woman next to her was Van's mother, and his son was there, too, and a niece, and they were waiting for a few more. Everyone had come by to tell me about Van.

For a second, I didn't even recognize him. He looked so different than when I'd seen him in the clinic, now happier and relaxed, surrounded by his family. He was wearing a vest to hold his batteries, and I could see the bulge under his white T-shirt where the controller sat, but only if I looked closely. I settled into my seat and introduced myself to the group while Van ducked into the kitchen to pull a steaming plate of baked potatoes, chives, and sour cream out of the oven. He'd found the recipe on Facebook and was excited for us to try it. Since the VAD, he explained to me via the pass-through from the kitchen, he'd learned to surf the Internet, and Facebook was one of his favorite sites to visit.

The VAD's batteries would run out of juice after twelve hours. That meant that each night, Van connected his controller to a power module that plugged into a wall socket so his batteries could recharge. Plugged into the wall at night, he was limited to the cord's twenty-foot radius, "like a dog on a leash," until the morning, when he could disconnect from the wall and plug the controller back into the newly charged batteries. Luckily, his house was small enough so that he could make it from the bedroom to the kitchen even when he was plugged in. The bathroom was even closer.

On the morning I visited, his wake-up alarm had gone off at 4 a.m. The day kicked off with a shower. Even after three years with the VAD, he still hadn't acclimated to the process. To start, the batteries and controller must stay dry, so he had to take the batteries from their holster and the controller from the Velcro belt Donna sewed for him, and place them all in a large waterproof shower bag that was specifically designed for showering with a battery-operated heart. The bag sealed on top, and the cord and wires exited through a hole in the plastic. This all went into another bag, which was also sealed on top, for extra protection. His doctors had suggested time limits for his showers—no longer than ten minutes, two times a week. The equipment was safer that way. He followed those instructions, mostly, but sometimes he just needed the feeling of that third shower, so he took it.

After the shower, it took time to change the dressing that covered the hole in his abdomen where the cable entered his body. This part was fairly simple. I walked with Van into his room, and he showed me the corner where he kept a pile of dressing change kits on a shelf. When he first came home from the hospital, he followed his doctor's directions perfectly. He didn't really have a choice. He wasn't allowed to be on his own in those early days in case he faced an emergency with his device—some VAD programs won't even consider placing a VAD in a patient who doesn't have a willing caregiver—so one of his sisters or his daughter stayed with him each day and night. While Van was in the hospital, each member of the family had been trained in how to clean the dressing and change the VAD batteries. They'd practiced what to do if the device started to sound its shrill alarm, repeating the steps again and again in the hope that muscle memory might overcome panic. Even Darlene, who was squeamish around medical procedures, learned how to change the dressing that covered the spot where the driveline entered Van's stomach.

So when he'd first returned home, Van allowed his family members to stay with him, and together they would change his dressings exactly as they'd been taught, carefully following each of the steps. They would bring the supplies over to Van's bed. He would lie down and rub alcohol wipes at the site for three to four minutes to loosen the bandage. Then one of his sisters, or whoever was with him, would remove the bandage slowly, inspecting the spot where the driveline entered the skin. Often, there was a bit of dry reddish crust, and they cleaned this off with alcohol and then saline. That would take fifteen minutes. Van would wait another fifteen minutes for his skin to dry, and then cover it back up with another dressing.

By the time we met, he had taken to doing the dressing changes on his own, and sometimes he cut a few corners, he told me with a shrug, for example pulling the bandage off before rubbing it down with alcohol. Even so, he had to be careful and deliberate. Including the breaks Van needed in order to relax and catch his breath, the shower plus dressing change was about a three-hour ordeal. Usually, after a rest, Van sipped his coffee while playing a few rounds of solitaire on his computer. He liked to stay busy. On the day I stopped by, he had spent the morning making food for my visit. After the potatoes, there would be a tray of brownies with strawberries and whipped cream, and he mentioned that he hoped we would leave room for the dessert.

As we talked, the front door swung open. I heard a child's high-pitched voice and turned around to meet Van's daughter and her son, his grandson, a round-faced four-year-old named Dylan who burst into the house in a Superman T-shirt. He ran toward Van, excited to see his grandfather, and gave him a huge hug. A few months after Van returned home from the hospital, his daughter had called him to ask if he wanted to watch Dylan. Van adored that little boy, kept a picture of him on the fridge, and savored their time together, but he had said no. He was scared something would happen, that his device would malfunction and he would pass out and the little boy, who was a toddler at the time, would be terrified and, unsupervised, could even get hurt. At first, he would only watch Dylan when his mother or one of his sisters was in the house along with him.

"If I fainted or something, what was he going to do? Just wait in the house alone all day until someone found him?" He explained his fears to me as I stood by the kitchen while Dylan ran around the living room. "The life was new.

I had to readjust to the life." As the months and then years passed, he grew comfortable enough to spend some hours alone with his grandson, but still with family backup programmed on his speed dial. He hadn't shaken the specter of device malfunction and possible catastrophe. "When me and him are alone—it's always on my mind," he told me.

One time, Van woke at 2 a.m. to the sound of a loud beep. Thinking there might be something wrong with his VAD, he changed his connection from the wall unit to a set of batteries. The sound continued. Though he wasn't supposed to switch controllers without explicit instructions from his doctors, he was frustrated, and it was the middle of the night. So he fiddled around with the machine, doing things he definitely wasn't supposed to do, and still the noise wouldn't stop. He dragged himself out of bed and to his phone to call his VAD team. Only when he got to the phone and saw the receiver hanging off the hook did Van realize the source of the noise— it was the phone and not his VAD after all. As he told the story, the assembled family members laughed appreciatively, although they'd heard it before. I found myself laughing, too, forgetting briefly that he was talking about life or death, about mistaking the sound of a phone off the hook for a sound that could have meant he was moments away from collapse.

As the laughter quieted, there was a break in our conversation. In the moment of stillness, I found that I was curious about Van's pulse. I asked him if I could feel for it, and, seemingly amused, he offered his hand. I placed my fingers on his wrist, where I am used to feeling the rhythmic pulsations of the radial artery. Because the device moved blood through Van's vessels at a continuous, stable rate of flow rather than the pumping of a normal heart, I couldn't feel a thing. It was somewhat disconcerting, I admitted, and Van smiled. He and his family joked about this kind of stuff. When Van got on his sisters' nerves, they liked to tell him that he'd better behave or else they would unplug him.

At first the goal had been to get Van a new heart. His doctors had told him that a transplant might be possible (his device could be termed a "bridge to decision") but that he would have to wait because he'd been smoking cigarettes right up until he got his VAD. Van wanted a transplant, or at least he thought he did. A transplant would allow him to live without batteries and, perhaps more important for him, would let him go swimming and teach his grandson how to fish. For the early months after the device was implanted, he returned to the clinic every two weeks so that his doctors could check the machine and continue the work-up to see if he could become a candidate for a new heart. Donna generally did the driving, and it took at least an hour each way on a good day. As much as the frequent doctor visits, the hours on the road and in the waiting room, and the promise of test after test chafed, Van stuck with it.

It seemed to pay off. He was ultimately listed for a transplant, but as he waited for his organ to come, his emphysema began to take center stage. He hadn't smoked a cigarette since before the hospital stay when he got the

VAD, and he puffed on his inhalers twice a day, but his lung function continued to decline. He was still too winded to get back to work, not because of his heart now but because of his lungs. And he learned that if his lungs didn't improve, he might not be able to get a new heart after all. He went to more appointments, refilled more prescriptions. He saw a new pulmonologist who reviewed his records and told him, simply, that there was nothing he could do to help. Van was frustrated and angry, but he couldn't change the facts, and at a clinic visit his doctors gave him the news: There would be no heart transplant. He would receive an official letter a few weeks later. "They decided I was off the list," Van told me with a shrug.

Donna took the news hard. She was devastated. She had been with Van through everything. She had kept a diary of the events of his hospital stay and had essentially lived at the hospital with him during the long days and nights of complications after he got the VAD, when he had to return to the OR and she was afraid that he might die. She'd driven him into Boston for his clinic appointments and had sat at the wheel one evening when his controller kept beeping and they had to rush to the hospital to figure out why. Despite all of that, he was off the list and there was nothing she could do. "It was a tough couple of days even for me to accept it," she told me of the transplant decision.

But Van reacted differently. He was not the sort to dwell on things, nor was he a man who allowed himself to wallow in feelings of regret. He didn't want to wish for something that wouldn't come, only to end up disappointed. I asked him what it was like to learn that he would spend the rest of his life with this machine, that the equipment would be with him until he died, and that he would never be able to shower the way he liked or go fishing. I wanted to know if it had been hard to come to terms with this. To the contrary, he told me. When the transplant was a possibility, he'd been at the beck and call of the clinic. He had to drive in for tests when they told him to. They'd even forced him to get a colonoscopy. He had wanted a new heart so that he could hunt and he could fish, but that wasn't going to happen. Without the uncertainty of a different future that might never come to pass, he could focus on accepting his life for what it was. "It was the best thing they did," he said of being taken off the transplant list. Sure, he still had to come into Boston every few months, but it was as if a cord had been cut, and in a way he was free. "It had come to the point where they were controlling my life," Van said. "They owned me, and I don't like being owned by anyone. Now I could live."

A few weeks after he learned that he would not get a heart transplant, he decided to go to the beach with his family. It would be the first trip he'd taken with the machine. He and his family rented seven rooms in a hotel by the water in Maine. They had a cookout one night, all of them, Van and his mother and his sisters and his kids and their children, warmed by the sun and the breeze off the ocean. It was a good weekend.

Perhaps I'd gotten it wrong. I had thought of life with the

device as a kind of purgatory. For some, this is the case. I had spoken with another patient who lived with a VAD until he received a heart transplant, and he told me that every night when he had the VAD, he prayed that he'd wake up in the morning, and every morning, he prayed he'd make it through the day. He didn't hate the VAD itself, he'd made his peace with it, but he found himself tortured by this external reminder of his mortality. He knew he was being kept alive by a machine, he could touch it and feel it, and he knew, too, that machines break. He could think of little else. Yet for Van, purgatory wasn't the cord that led from his chest to his battery pack. It wasn't the prospect of life with a VAD without the promise of transplant. It wasn't the idea of the alarms that could awaken him at night. For Van, it was the waiting, that and being tied to the clinic. In contrast to what I would have assumed, that had been the worst part.

Back when he got the device, Van asked his doctors how long he could be expected to live with it. At that time, their longest-living patient had gone for seven years. When we met, it had been three years since his own machine had been implanted, but Van didn't seem too focused on counting down the time. He hadn't expected any of this to happen—not the heart failure, and surely not the idea that he would be living with a VAD—and now that it had, he didn't know how long the pump and the batteries and the controller would continue to give him the life that he wanted. It would be good to have more years. He could spend time with his grandson and get to know the boy as he grew up. He could continue to have fun with his sisters, crashing their girls'-night-out dinners. But the limitations of current technology made the future feel especially uncertain. Perhaps it was his time in AA, but somehow he was able to recognize this unknown without being paralyzed by it. And then he could move on.

"I don't care if I die today. I live each day for each day," he told me over the phone one morning. After I visited Van at his home, we had continued to talk on the phone from time to time. In the midst of our conversation that morning, he got a call from the clinic updating him on his labs; the dosage of his blood thinner could remain stable for the week. "This isn't even about me anymore. This is about the whole family. A lot of people have put a lot of hours and a lot of effort into keeping me alive. I'm going to enjoy it."

And he had been enjoying it. With the power of the VAD, Van had been able to return to the camper he'd started before his health went downhill. Working a little bit each day, he used plywood to build the camper's body, eight feet long, four feet wide, and four feet high. He put in windows, an air conditioner, and two doors, and he covered it all with plastic siding. A few weeks after he finished, Van, his mother, his sister Donna, and her husband piled into his minivan with the camper hitched to the back, to travel up to his brother's house in the White Mountains in New Hampshire. He brought his battery charger with him and carried a generator, too, in case he needed to charge while he was on the road. He stayed on battery the whole weekend rather than plugging into the wall at night, opting instead to make sure he changed his drained batteries for fresh ones every twelve hours. This let him sleep outside, in the camper he had built. It was peaceful out there, and he slept easily. It was, he said, a "pretty decent" time.

"Sometimes you have a good day, sometimes you have a bad day," he said during another phone call, when I asked him how he was doing. I had come to look forward to Van's calls. I found myself trying to see his life the way he did, without that anxious need to know what was going to happen or the inclination to look over his shoulder with regret. On that day things were good, "better than good, wonderful, even," he told me, and I was surprised to hear him sound almost effusive. He had recently decided to start working out and had picked up an exercise bench, which he used to lift weights. For some cardio, he had honed a routine of jumping jacks without jumping and twists from the waist. Already he had lost weight and felt that he could move around better. In fact, when we talked, he had gone to see his pulmonologist a few days before and had learned that his lung function had actually been improving. I thought immediately of transplant when he told me that, wondering if the option could come back on the table. Hesitantly, I asked whether that was on his mind, too. "It's always a possibility," he acknowledged. "But I'm not going to wrap my life around it. It's been so long now, I'm fine just the way I am."

He had even gone on a few dinner dates since the VAD was placed. He wanted to meet someone, but struggled with the best way to explain his device to women. "When they find out I'm running around with batteries, they kind of shy away," he told me with a chuckle. It occurred to me, as we talked about exercise and dating attempts, that even in the course of the months we had known each other, Van had changed. I wondered if part of this increasing positivity was his shifting relationship with the realities of the VAD. I asked him about this, and he agreed. "It's just a part of my life now, it's an everyday thing," he said, referring to the VAD. "I'm more comfortable with it, and that's it, you know?"

This sense of comfort had allowed him to start working on another project. The camper complete, he had decided to fix up a fourteen-foot speedboat that he would use to go fishing on a lake near his home. It was a big lake, some twenty-six miles across, and it could be tough to catch fish there because you had to know where they were hiding. Van had learned to fish as a child with his father and siblings. They'd spend the days outside, boating and fishing, and the nights camping. Van's father would bring his guitar, and the family would have a sing-along around the fire. It was a good way to grow up and a tradition he had tried to replicate for his own children. Years had passed since he had last gone fishing; his doctors had warned him time and time again about getting too close to bodies of water with the VAD. But when the summer came, he would re-learn the best spots in the lake. He would drop his fishing line out of the boat, throw his feet over the side, and re-lax and enjoy the day. He'd come home with some salmon or rainbow trout or perch, and cook the fish on his George Foreman grill. He'd picked up a little fishing pole for his grandson, too. He wanted to teach Dylan to fish, but he would make sure someone else came along, too, for safety. I had rarely heard him this animated. And I began to un-derstand that it was worth it for him to loosen his shackles and break the rules.

"If I'm just going to sit and live in fear, I'd rather be dead. I'll take my chances," he told me over the phone. "Life as I know it, it's how it is right now. When the pump goes down, I go down. When you unplug me, I go down. But I don't have time to worry about all that." It had been more than five years since his heart had started to fail and over a year since he'd been told he wouldn't get a heart transplant. He had a hole in his stomach and a vest to carry his batteries and the elastic band his sister had fashioned to hold the controller around his waist and the ever-present threat of a stroke or a bleed or a problem with the machine. Most likely, there would be no transplant. This was the way that he was going to live until he got sick, or until some-thing was broken that could not be fixed. There are those who might not choose this route, but when faced with a set of ultimately unimaginable alternatives, Van had. And that afternoon, he was going to take a quick rest, and then, if the weather held up, he was going to take a ride to Walmart. I smiled when he told me what he was planning to get there—rope, an anchor, another life jacket, and a horn. Summer was coming, and Van wanted to be ready to take his grandson fishing.

4

Nightmares After the ICU

It was time for our morning exam. We clustered around
the bed to observe our patient. His face was puffy from
fluids, and he was tethered to the bed by plastic tubing,
soft restraints, and intravenous lines. One of the other residents placed a stethoscope on his chest, listened to the
sounds of his heart and his lungs, and nodded. Better every day. I laid my hand on his abdomen and pushed gently.
The man's eyes darted and his body contorted as he struggled to free his arms from the restraints and move them
toward his breathing tube. I reached reflexively, grabbed
his hand, and pressed it firmly down into the bed. He grimaced.

I turned to address his wife, who was standing in the
doorway. We had grown used to her presence over the past
few weeks. In the beginning, when bacteria flooded her
husband's body and we were unsure whether he would live
or die, she had barely left his bedside. She must have said
goodbye to him on that first night, and if not then, surely
the night after, when one of the interns whispered her

name into the darkness of the small hot family room where she was half sleeping to tell her that her husband's oxygen levels were dropping. In those early days, he was the first patient we saw on our morning rounds and the last patient we examined before leaving the hospital for the night.

But the days passed, and slowly he started to get better. Sicker patients took his place in our morning rounding order. Now he was close to being able to breathe without the ventilator. He was clearly delirious—when he woke, it was to flail in the bed and only intermittently follow our instructions. I didn't focus on that, though; he would not die, nor would he linger in the purgatory of long-term ventilator dependence. This patient was lucky. He would leave the hospital weak but alive and intact, breathing on his own, without question a "save."

Yet for my patient, it was far from over. In his mind, I learned much later, he had spent the days since his intubation railing against invisible captors. He believed that his house had been burned to the ground and his children made to work as slaves. He felt himself to be hog-tied, naked and cold. He saw blood dripping down the walls. These images would follow him from the intensive care unit to the general medical floor and out of the hospital to his home, where they would come to him unbidden as nightmares when he tried to sleep and as flashbacks during the day.

"Looks like he'll be able to breathe without the tube soon. We're hoping to be able to take it out tomorrow," I told his wife. She sighed, relieved. "Did you hear that?" She looked toward her husband, who was kicking his legs under the hospital sheets. "The tube is going to come out!" She turned back to me. "He's going to be okay," she said slowly, as if savoring the sound of the words. I nodded. I didn't have an inkling of the battle that was being waged in his mind, nor did I have any idea of how that might change him. I didn't wonder whether he would be able to return to work, how long it would take to get to that point, and what his life might be like if he could not. He would be okay. That was the truth, as far as I knew it. And it would remain that way until I met a woman named Nancy Andrews.

It was the early 1980s in Baltimore, more than two decades before I ever set foot in an ICU, and a twenty-year-old art student named Nancy Andrews needed an eye exam to get a new pair of glasses. Strapped for cash, she headed to the ophthalmology clinic at Johns Hopkins, where she'd heard she could get her eyes examined by a doctor in training for as little as thirty dollars. The doctor there peered into her eyes, looking behind her pupils at her lenses. Oddly, it appeared as though they had shifted from their expected location.

"Your lenses are dislocated," he said. Had she ever been hit over the head? That would be a convenient explanation for dislocated lenses. She hadn't. The young doctor looked at his patient, taking in her slender build, her long fingers, her flexible wrists. There was something more going on.

At the end of the day, Nancy found herself at the hospital's genetics center awaiting a diagnosis. When it finally came, it confirmed the suspicion that had troubled the doctor at the eye clinic: Nancy had Marfan syndrome.

Marfan's—named for French pediatrician Antoine Marfan, who first described the condition at the turn of the twentieth century in a young girl with long fingers and skeletal abnormalities—is a disorder of the connective tissue that holds together the body's skin, muscles, and organs. Those with this diagnosis are prone to problems that range from the relatively benign, like lens dislocations in the eye, to deadly defects of the aorta, the large vessel that carries blood from the heart to the rest of the body. Nancy was quickly subjected to test after test. As if the diagnosis itself weren't jarring enough, she then learned that she had an aneurysm at the base of her aorta. If left unaddressed, Nancy's doctor warned her, the weakened vessel could rupture with disastrous, and potentially fatal, consequences.

She felt completely healthy. She was active. She rode her bike all around the city and even had enough energy to work an extra job washing dishes. Now, with this diagnosis, her good health was just an illusion. Shaken, Nancy asked her doctor how he suggested she make sense of the seismic shift in her reality. He told her that any of us could die at any moment, really. "This is different," she replied. "You're telling me I have a ticking time bomb in me." She didn't get an answer.

With a prescription for blood pressure meds to keep the growth of the aneurysm in check, she carried on. What other choice did she have? As planned, she traveled to England for the year to study. But when she returned to Hopkins in the fall, she saw her doctor again. He told her that the aneurysm had now grown large enough that the benefits of surgery to repair it outweighed the risk. So at twenty-one, Nancy agreed to undergo open-heart surgery to replace the diseased root of her aorta and her aortic valve with a polyester graft and a plastic and metal prosthesis.

Faced with the fear of a massive surgery, Nancy turned to art. She shot photos of herself on the way down the hall to the OR and then again in the mirror after the surgery and throughout her convalescence. Recovery was rough, but she was young and healthy, and slowly re-gained the strength to return to the eclectic fun of her everyday life. She finished college, using the surgical photos as her senior project. Sure, she had a genetic con-dition that wasn't going away, and there was the looming threat of another surgery, and when she went in to see her doctors they paraded her in front of the medical students like some kind of sideshow attraction, but in her day-to-day, Nancy was okay. She was an artist in her twenties, playing the violin and singing in an avant-garde perfor-mance group. She found a day job working as a video producer on a hospital television channel, where she cre-ated programs like hospital bingo for sick children. As the years went by, she developed a serious interest in experi-mental film, which led her from Baltimore to Chicago to pursue an advanced degree, and then on to a job as an art professor in coastal Maine. Two decades passed. All the while, she returned annually to Hopkins to monitor the rest of her aorta, which was slowly but certainly growing in size. She wore a medical alert bracelet reading "At risk for aortic dissection." The vessel would have to be repaired—a complex surgery that would put Nancy at risk for paralysis, kidney failure, even death—and it wasn't a question of *if* but *when*.

Nancy asked her doctors what it would feel like if the wall in her aorta tore before it came time to repair. Depending on where the aorta dissects, this is a surgical emergency that, untreated, can quickly lead to death. Nancy learned that her impending death would feel like intense lower back pain. She filed this information away in the back of her mind, where it stayed until one autumn morning in 2005.

Nancy was waiting at her local clinic for a regular blood draw, a necessity since she was on blood thinners to prevent clots in her artificial aortic valve, when her back started to bother her. At first, she thought it might be the plastic chair she'd been sitting in. She moved around, stood up, and sat back down again, but the pain didn't subside. There was something different about this pain, a gripping quality that crept into the margins of her consciousness and didn't let up. It intensified. "I think I'm having an aortic dissection," she remembers telling the clerk at the front desk of the clinic waiting room. "Could you call an ambulance?"

From there on, her memories are vague. Nancy remembers collapsing. She remembers an ambulance racing from the little town clinic to the nearest regional hospital in Bangor, Maine, and the helicopter that brought her to Brigham and Women's Hospital in Boston. She remembers that the medical crew in the helicopter put a headset on her and told her that she could use it to communicate, like Madonna in concert. In the operating room, surgeons made a vertical incision from below her navel up to her chest, under her breast, and around her back so they could begin work on her aorta. By the time she emerged, most of the ruptured vessel had been replaced with polyester. She had lived.

With sedatives running through her veins, Nancy's body was quiet. But her mind raced, creating explanations for the inexplicable. She was at the bottom of a boat or trapped in a deep well. Seven-eighths of her brain had been removed. Hospital staff wanted to kill her. When her team of doctors came in each morning to ask her the basic orientation questions—her name, the date, where she was—she believed the questions were a test and she would be liberated from her imprisonment if she passed. On other days, she had uncovered a porn ring that took pictures of hospitalized patients and put them on the Internet. The sound of a drawer shutting was a person being shot in the hallway. The images were vivid, themes of traveling through the desert, of struggling to survive in Arctic landscapes. Her family members sat at her bedside, unaware of the depth of her paranoid confusion. But as Nancy slowly became strong enough to talk and write, pieces of the complicated nightmare inside her mind began to surface.

When friends visited, she asked them to wipe the insects off their faces. She scrawled desperate messages to tell someone, anyone, that a part of her brain had been cut away. Her partner asked the doctors and nurses over and over again, "What's wrong with her? Is this normal?" It was disconcerting. She knew that Nancy had survived a physically grueling surgery and could see that her chest was healing, but what was going on with her mind? The doctors didn't seem to think much of it. "Oh yeah, that happens," they responded, as though it had no real import. Her medical team seemed confident that by the time she made it home, her mind would have returned to normal.

But even when the delirium seemed to have passed and Nancy was strong enough to leave the hospital (first for a rehabilitation facility and then for her home on the Maine coast), she wasn't the same. At rehab in Bangor, she heard a helicopter and found herself mysteriously brought to tears. Back at home, one night friends came over for dinner with their baby. The parents made airplane noises as they brought spoonfuls of food to the child's mouth, and something about the seemingly innocuous activity led Nancy to panic. "My every instinct was to hit the deck," she remembered, only later connecting the dots between her reaction and her medical helicopter trip from Maine to Boston. "I wanted to cower." At a documentary film seminar program, she found herself entirely confused by the language of film critique that used to come easily to her. Her mind felt muddy. She couldn't shake the belief that something else was wrong—something beyond the expected challenges of her physical recovery. A smell would suddenly conjure up images of torture, of people tied to beds, of blood and insects and suffering. It was as though she were haunted. "It was shocking, and I didn't know what was happening," she told me. The doctors who had operated on her aorta had been thrilled just to know that she was alive. But she was now forty-four years old. As grateful as she was to them, she couldn't stand to think that she would live out her remaining decades this way, scared and confused, broken.

At an appointment with her long-term primary care doctor a few months after her discharge from the hospital, Nancy decided to open up about her suffering. She was vague, uncertain how to explain what was going on. She told him a few things, like the way a smell could suddenly cause her to panic. As he listened to his patient, the former military man recognized a pattern. This sounded like post-traumatic stress disorder, but instead of having flashbacks to real traumatic events, Nancy was having flashbacks to hallucinatory experiences she had believed were real while she was delirious in the hospital. Of course, Nancy knew about PTSD. She knew that veterans of war could relive their traumas. But it had never occurred to her that this was something that could afflict an art professor who'd recently undergone a long and complicated hospital course. When she searched online to learn more, she mainly found information about PTSD among those who'd been in the military. Yet the more she considered it, the more sense the diagnosis made. It brought together some of the disparate pieces of her experience and gave them a name. It even gave her hope for a treatment plan. Soon after, eager to find a way to reenter her life, Nancy started seeing a therapist to begin an intensive program that would last for years.

One winter evening nearly a decade later, I was running late. It had been a long day in the intensive care unit, where I was on as the critical care fellow. We'd started the morning on time, but then a sick new admission had arrived in the middle of rounds with barely any medical records. We had to figure out who she was and why she had been airlifted to us from a hospital on Cape Cod, and then we still had to see the rest of the patients to set up their plans for the day. By the time we finished rounds, it was nearly 2 p.m. and we were ravenous. I left the residents to the now-cold pizza that had been waiting for them in their workroom while I went off to answer a page. It was the nurse manager, calling to alert us that there were two patients in the ER who had already been intubated and would definitely need ICU beds. She talked quickly. We would have to scramble to make room in the unit by sending our least sick patients out to the general medical floor. I interrupted the residents with the news, which sent the interns scurrying about for the next few hours, hastily composing transfer summaries for delirious patients who had been in the unit for days but had suddenly been deemed healthy enough to leave because of the bed crunch. I didn't even know what time it was until I saw the night shift nurses marching in, wearing scrubs and rain jackets (it was raining outside? Without any windows in the ICU, I had no idea), and toting the bags of food that would get them through till morning. I glanced at my watch. It was nearly 7 p.m., and I was going to be late for dinner.

Maybe I should cancel. I imagined going home, taking a shower, watching Netflix, and dining on my favorite weekday combination of cereal and wine. That was all I, achingly tired from a stretch of twelve-hour days in the unit, wanted to do. I definitely didn't want to walk through the dark, damp cold of a Boston winter to have dinner with a stranger. Besides, I wasn't even sure why I was meeting Nancy Andrews in the first place. It had happened on a whim. I was skimming through recent critical care papers one night, searching for something new to talk about in our daily morning lecture, when I stumbled upon an article describing the problems people face after critical illness. Though I didn't know it at the time, momentum had been building behind research showing that ICU survivors, even the ones who had made it home and appeared unimpaired, frequently struggled with psychological and cognitive issues they hadn't suffered before their intensive care hospitalization. Some developed PTSD, with flashbacks to horrifying delirium-induced delusions of severed limbs, sexual trauma, drowning, and torture. Others were anxious, depressed. Young people were left with memory problems that were similar to mild dementia. This constellation of problems—PTSD, depression, and cognitive dysfunction among them—even had a name: post–intensive care syndrome. Although doctors didn't know precisely who was at greatest risk, they did know that those who were delirious while critically ill, which had long struck me as an entirely benign condition, seemed more likely to develop these problems than those whose minds remained clear.

This was all news to me. When I was an intern, mortality was the only ICU outcome generally taught to doctors in training. The term "post–intensive care syndrome," or PICS, hadn't even been coined until 2010, two years after my internship ended. So while I'd learned the intricacies of ventilator settings in my intensive care rotations, we had never talked about the dysfunction that might come afterward. Reading about PICS that night years later, I still wasn't quite sure what, if anything, to do with this new knowledge. I had already come face-to-face with chronic critical illness, the ventilator-dependent survivors who had first forced me to question the "success" paradigm of our intensive care interventions. Now it seemed that even our best outcomes might lead to unanticipated and perhaps unavoidable harm. Knowing that I would return to the unit the next morning, I didn't want to pause too long to consider those facts. So I might have simply moved on to the next set of articles, hoping for something more sterile and less human, like antibiotics or ventilators, had I not come across a collection of haunting black-and-white sketches. In one, disembodied heads circled a banner that read "I Like Morphine." In another, a creature that appeared to be half human, half bird, with a scar along its chest, floated above a sketch of a hospital bed. They were fascinating, simple but captivating windows into the chaos of a delirious mind. What grabbed me even more was that the artist, a woman who'd survived an aortic dissection, had been treated at my own hospital.

When Nancy Andrews had first returned home, she had been too weak to hold her camera. She wasn't certain she would ever be able, or even want, to return to making films. But she could hold a pencil. Slowly, starting with squiggles, which were all that she could manage to create from her bed, Nancy had started to draw. And as her strength improved—and she began to feel motivated to share her experience—she kept drawing. She built a website, too, with links to her sketches and to articles about post-traumatic stress after critical illness and the lasting effects of delirium, and left an invitation for visitors to share their own stories or to contact her. Entranced by her artwork, I sent her a message. We made plans to meet for dinner at a restaurant near the hospital the next time Nancy came down to Boston.

By the time I made it to the Thai spot we'd picked, Nancy was already seated and waiting for me. I didn't know quite what I thought I might find, but it wasn't this thoughtful, articulate woman in thick-rimmed glasses, a patterned blazer, jeans, and funky sneakers. Perhaps I was surprised that she didn't look more wounded. Though I had taken care of countless patients who would become ICU survivors, and by that point had done my fair share of reading about post–intensive care syndrome, Nancy was the first to talk with me about that experience. As she told her story, I felt that tingle you get when you learn something new that might change you; I took notes furiously so I wouldn't miss a thing. I had no idea how many people I'd triumphantly helped carry back from the brink of death only to return them to their lives riddled with the invisible wounds that were now called PICS. We would declare them better, we would say they were healed enough to leave the unit, and then their outpatient doctors would applaud their progress in follow-up clinics. "You look great!" they'd say. In fact, I'd spoken those overly bright words to the patients we were hastily moving out of the unit earlier that same evening. But what we didn't acknowledge was that some of these ICU survivors wouldn't ever be able to get back to work, and some of their families would break under the struggle of sickness and caregiving and the stress of expanding piles of medical bills. I wondered how many of them would stay silent, afraid of being seen as weak or ungrateful or even crazy.

Nancy described herself to me as the "luckiest unlucky person." She was lucky to have had her eyes examined that day at Hopkins. She was lucky that her aorta tore in a clinic waiting room and that she knew the signs. She was lucky that she had a doctor who suspected she might have PTSD though it wasn't generally recognized as a complication of critical illness at the time. Yet when she shared her story with her other doctors in the years directly after her surgery, Nancy came up against a gap between common medical knowledge and her reality. At an early follow-up with her surgeon, she mentioned that she had been diagnosed with PTSD. "PTS-what?" he exclaimed, genuinely confused. With her scars hidden under her shirt, it was hard for Nancy to explain that she wasn't the same. "People couldn't see, really, what was wrong," she told me. "They could see when I was still using a cane. But people can't see the psychological scars." And perhaps, in a way, they didn't want to. "Really, the narrative people want to hear is that I'm all better, happy to be alive, and thankful," she explained. "No one wants to hear the dark side of it. But those things coexist."

As Nancy talked, I couldn't help but flash back to my current patients, intubated and sedated, anxious families at the bedside. I wondered if I should stop by each room the next morning after rounds and relay all I had learned, so that they would not be surprised when their recoveries didn't meet their hopeful expectations. And yet it seemed uncomfortable, and in a way thoughtless, to warn a husband that his wife might be forgetful or anxious or depressed just as she emerged from days on a ventilator. What was he to do with that information? Critical care had created a new syndrome, but it didn't come with any simple solution. So at home that night, back in the unit the next day, and in the months to come, I was quiet, uncertain how I might integrate this perspective into the daily realities of my life in the ICU.

It was night in the intensive care unit, and I was a few hours into an overnight shift. One woman on my patient list had been admitted with septic shock from pneumonia. She'd been intubated and was dangerously sick at first, but a week had passed, and now her blood pressure was holding steady and she was close to breathing on her own. I'd been called to her room for something minor, and when I entered, I saw the woman's daughter sitting at her bedside. She looked exhausted, and I wondered when she'd last allowed herself a full night's sleep.

I introduced myself as the doctor working overnight and told her that I was just going to take a look at the settings on her mother's ventilator. I said all this to the patient, too, although I did not know how much she would remember and carry with her, especially as her eyes were closed and sedating and pain-relieving medication flowed into her veins. I explained to her why I was there. I told her she was doing better, and I hoped that in the next day or two she would be able to breathe without the tube. When I finished, I looked toward her daughter, who had of course been listening. "I was so scared. I thought I was going to lose her. But she's going to be okay?" she said, her voice inflecting up at the end into a question.

There it was. I had heard that question so many times, ending with that same word, "okay." I had said the same thing myself. In a way, it was an easy kind of shorthand. And yet I had rarely paused to ask a key question of my own in response: What does it actually mean to be okay? The more I looked, the more complicated that answer had become. Since meeting Nancy Andrews, I'd started a new clinic at my hospital specifically for post-ICU patients. Though the idea was attractive, the reality had been slow going. Simply scheduling people for a clinic was harder than I had assumed. Even those who ultimately made it home often did so after multiple transitions, weeks to months winding through rehabs and nursing facilities. And these were people with terrifying memories of what had happened to them in the hospital, people who might not be willing to return for yet another subspecialist appointment or who were too weak to travel even if they had wanted to. Others might be cognitively impaired, with memory deficits that left them unable to remember the timing of the appointment or why they would even come to our clinic in the first place.

But we had seen a handful of patients so far. We sorted through meds and screened for common post-ICU issues through questionnaires and conversations. A former EMT told me he didn't want to spend time alone with his young son because he was afraid that he and the boy would be attacked—by what or whom, he couldn't say—and he wouldn't react quickly enough. Another patient admitted that she was afraid to cook, worried that she would turn the oven on, forget, and return hours later to find her food charred and smoking. In response, we listened, arranged subspecialist referrals, and summarized our findings in a note that would travel to each person's outpatient doctors, so that we might begin to bridge the chasm that separated what had happened in the intensive care unit from what came afterward. But perhaps most important, we talked about post–intensive care syndrome. We gave our patients a name and a diagnosis, and with that, I think, a degree of reassurance and perhaps even hope. That felt so small, compared to the interventions we delivered in the ICU, but it was something.

I stood in front of my patient that night, thinking of the question her daughter had asked, but also of the patients I had seen at the clinic. I thought of confusion and lost memories, sadness and overwhelming anxiety, nightmares and flashbacks to blood and carnage and suffering. In some ways, the people I had seen in our clinic were completely, unequivocally okay. These were the saves, the ones who had left the ICU and made it home. They could walk and talk, live with their families, go shopping, and eat the foods they wanted. But in other ways, compared to the lives they'd lived before critical illness, they weren't okay at all.

What new reality would this patient face? Maybe she would be okay, really okay. She would go to rehab—and that would be harder than I could imagine—but she would return to her world much as she'd left it. We are making changes in the ICU, like decreasing sedation and monitoring for delirium, and perhaps those interventions would make things better for her than they would have been otherwise. But even so, she might return home only to find her mind cloudy, her life in shadow. She might not be able to focus on the Sunday paper, or be able to spend time alone with her grandchildren, or even remember to go to the store to get milk. As the moonlighter, I didn't know enough about her to understand what her life had been like before. But I did know that it would be different moving forward.

I wondered if I should say any of this to her daughter. I gathered my thoughts and took a breath, preparing to speak, but then I stopped. Even if I told her daughter how things might be, even if I gave her the language of post–intensive care syndrome and told her what that might mean for her mother, I doubted that she would really be able to do anything with those words. She was so tired and so deeply relieved by the simple knowledge that her mother would not die in that room. That was all she wanted to hear. Maybe it was all she could hear, in that moment.

So I smiled and I nodded reassuringly. It was true. Her mother's breathing tube would come out, and she would leave the intensive care unit. And what then? I paused and jotted her name down so that I could find out how she was doing. Maybe I could make her an appointment in our clinic. I would try to remember to do so. For now, that would have to be enough.

5

Emergence

Andrea DeMayo-Clancy bustled about her comfortable kitchen. It was a scorching summer day outside, but inside it was pleasantly cool. The espresso machine hummed with the morning coffee. The family's dogs—two rescued from a puppy mill, the third adopted from a shelter—barked and begged underfoot. Andrea's middle child, twenty-year-old Greg, clumped down the stairs, muttered good morning, and grabbed a bagel from the fridge to take with him to his job at the local coffee roaster.

"Bring some more coffee home, would you?" Andrea called after him.

Greg mumbled an okay before heading out the door.

Amid all the movement of this ordinary morning, Ben Clancy was still.

Ben sat quietly at the kitchen table while a visiting nurse wrapped a blood pressure cuff around his upper arm and recorded the results in a small notepad. His heart rate and blood pressure were normal and stable. It was one of the last times a nurse would need to come see him at home.

At first glance, he looked like a healthy twenty-four-year-old guy, brown hair cropped close to his head, dressed in a Boston T-shirt, plaid shorts, and running shoes. But there was something about the stillness—even before Ben got up to practice walking and faltered for an instant, his physical therapist grabbing his belt to support him—that hinted at the events that had thrust him and his family into the murky world of recovery from brain injury.

It had been just over five months since the overdose that had caused Ben's heart to stop. When his eyes had first opened afterward, his gaze appeared empty and un-comprehending. Now there were pockets of blankness and confusion where memories had once resided, but he was home. He passed the time pleasantly with his mother, watching television and laughing at the shows when they were funny. And it had only been five months. He would keep getting better. That much seemed clear. But "better" is such a vague word. Does it mean that Ben will be able to live on his own and drive a car to work and go out on a date on a Friday night? Or does it mean something more modest, like walking without someone there to catch his fall, remembering to make lunch, turning the stove on and off again, and maybe putting away the dishes?

Brain injury is a relatively young field of study, with new diagnostic categories and methods of tracking progress. Neurology researchers now know that significant improvement can occur over years, which is heartening, yet potentially torturous for families awaiting change that might or might not come. This is the mystery of brain injury, and what led me to the Clancy kitchen that morning. How much of the essential essence of Ben—that big, booming laugh that could fill a room, the flirtation and charisma, quick wit and intellect—lay dormant but would one day return, and how much of it was gone forever?

When we met, I asked Ben's mother what she was hoping for, and Andrea told me, without hesitation, "Everything." She knew that things would be different from the life that she had once imagined for her son. But when she closed her eyes and let herself look into the future, she still saw Ben going to work each day at a job he enjoyed. He'd always told her he would drive a Ferrari, and maybe that wouldn't happen, but she imagined her boy as a man behind the wheel of his own car. The visiting nurse had been talking about a different set of goals, such as a group home and a simple job. That was probably more realistic, Andrea acknowledged, but she wasn't ready to see that as her son's future. It had been only a few months, and she was still hoping for something bigger.

Ben Clancy was a charmer. He could command a room. He was the guy who took the less popular stance in a debate just for the fun of it, just to be provocative, even if that meant defending a viewpoint he didn't necessarily believe. He'd been a high school athlete who played on the football team but also loved jazz guitar, and in his small independent school he was encouraged to pursue both.

Ben's parents, Andrea and Bryan, had built their house on a thirty-acre lot in a small town about half an hour from Boston, and it became the spot where Ben's large group of friends felt comfortable congregating. The Clancy house had enough extra rooms, warmth, and generosity that one of Ben's friends even moved in for a couple of months while he was working through some personal issues. It was just that kind of place—a "home to the lost boys," Andrea remembers.

It's not clear when Ben's partying crossed the line. He'd been excited to start college at a small liberal arts school on a lake in upstate New York. He joined a frat there and decided to major in public policy. By junior year his grades had plummeted, and his parents confronted him when he came home for winter break. They knew he'd been drinking to excess. He also admitted that he had been experimenting with prescription narcotics on campus. Of course college boys in a frat would drink, Ben's parents acknowledged that, but the drugs worried them.

"We were brutal about that," his mother remembers. "We told him, 'There's no more college. We're not writing a check for you to do that.'" Ben was furious, but his parents offered him no other choice. He could go back to school the following fall, but first he'd move home to spend the spring semester working on a construction site. Those were the terms. At the end of each day, Ben returned home exhausted, too tired from demolition and digging holes to have any interest in going out drinking or doing anything much at all, other than falling asleep. Andrea and Bryan felt hopeful. Their gamble seemed successful. After months of arduous physical labor, Ben appeared to have straightened out.

When he returned to college that fall, he hung up his hard hat in his dorm room, proud of his time away. He had been changed by it. He brought home stellar grades and completed his course work, out of sync with his peers, the winter after many of his friends had already earned their diplomas. When he finished his courses, Ben moved back into his parents' house while he started to look for a job. It must have been anticlimactic—he was done with college yet there he was, unemployed, living in his old bedroom, and he had to wait to officially graduate in the spring. Though it wasn't ideal, Ben and his parents assumed that his time at home would be a short stint. But as the months crept on, his relative lack of independence began to infuriate him. Ben felt as though he had to ask permission for everything, and he hated asking for money, even for something as simple as a ride on the train. Andrea knew how much living at home without an income bothered her independent son, but at the same time she worried about the drinking and the dabbling with prescription pills, and she didn't want to send him off with hundreds of dollars. So she gave him enough but not extra, and if he needed more, he'd have to ask for it. She didn't think she and her husband were too hard on him. They did not intend to be.

By the fall, some ten months after Ben had finished school, things had started to unravel. He still didn't have a job. Most of his friends had found work, and they were busy. Ben made new friends, people who were willing and able to party with him midweek, and when he wasn't with them, he drank alone in his room. It wasn't a question any longer—he had a problem. His parents sent him to see a counselor, but Ben didn't like what she had to say, so he stopped going. When Andrea and Bryan pushed him to go back, he assured them that his behavior would change once he started working. With the mandates of a regular schedule, he promised, things would get better. He was convincing. They all wanted this to be true.

Sure enough, after months of looking and waiting, and dozens of phone calls and voicemails leading to one disappointment after another, Ben got three offers. He had his pick, and he chose to work on the business development team of a new company dedicated to improving energy efficiency. It seemed like a promising first job, working toward a mission he believed in alongside a good group of colleagues. Ben set his start date for the last Monday in February. The weekend before, he went out to party with some friends in Boston.

It was early afternoon on Sunday. Andrea and Bryan hadn't heard from Ben since the day before, but he was out with his friends, so that was hardly unusual. Bryan was at home when his cell phone rang. It was about Ben. Something had happened. It was serious, and Ben was in the hospital in Boston. Andrea was at her daughter's school, in the middle of a dress rehearsal for their musical. She had been in charge of making the costumes. When her phone buzzed, she had no inkling of the magnitude of the situation, so she waited for a few minutes to sneak out during intermission.

She received the same message as her husband, left the theater, and headed straight to Massachusetts General Hospital. Bryan had arrived first and called Andrea with the details of where she should park and where they would meet. She didn't yet feel scared—she wasn't sure what to expect. When she arrived in the ER, a social worker met her in the waiting room and took her to her husband. Together, they went to see their son. He lay on a stretcher, hooked to a ventilator, unmoving, with cooling pads wrapped around his body.

Ben had been drinking and taking heroin and cocaine and sedatives, substances that, in a near fatal combination, had caused him to lose consciousness. His friends were likely too impaired themselves to notice what was going on at first. Someone had thought to call a relative, who might have been a nurse, early that morning, but it took some more time before they dialed 911, and by that point Ben had stopped breathing. Deprived of oxygen, his heart then stopped, too.

When they arrived, the paramedics performed CPR, attempting to restart Ben's heart with drugs and defibrillation. Though his heart was young and resilient and forgave the incident, his brain had been severely injured by the time without oxygen, and as a result, Ben didn't wake up. Andrea and Bryan learned that Ben's doctors were using the cooling pads to lower their son's body temperature in the hope of decreasing inflammation and cell death, thereby mitigating the damage that had been done to his brain. Ben was sedated and paralyzed, too, so that his body would tolerate the cold without shivering— which could cause discomfort and raise his temperature. Bryan and Andrea stood at his bedside. It was as though they, too, were frozen, watching.

Wow. He really did it this time. That was all Andrea could think. They had seen their share of Ben-related close calls. He'd been stopped once for driving after he had been drinking to excess. On another occasion, sober but exhausted, he'd fallen asleep at the wheel and sent his car hurtling a quarter mile off the highway down a fifty-foot embankment. The guy who found the car saw Ben walking, unharmed, and couldn't believe that he had been the one driving.

Both times, Ben had been lucky. But this was different. Andrea couldn't let her mind go any further, not wanting to imagine how she would feel if her son never woke up. Sitting at the bedside, numbly watching the doctors and nurses tend to Ben's body and the machines that were keeping it alive, Bryan contacted Ben's would-be employers. He left a message saying that Ben would not be starting work the next day as planned. He wouldn't be there the day after, either. Bryan later heard back from someone in the company who said that he, too, had been hospitalized with a brain injury a decade earlier. Other than still having some lasting problems with memory, he'd recovered. He told Ben's father that he'd be waiting to hear how Ben did.

Ben's doctors laid out their short-term goals—Ben would not die, they would rewarm him, they would turn off the meds that kept him paralyzed and sedated, and he would wake up. No one would say what might happen after that awakening or how much of Ben would remain. A day passed. As planned, the rewarming started, and Ben's body temperature ticked up toward normal, degree by degree. His doctors stopped the sedation, but Ben remained comatose. It was as though time moved in slow motion. Ben had undergone a CT scan of his head soon after the overdose to look for a bleed or a stroke; he'd experienced neither. Now, his doctors sent him for an MRI to gain a more nuanced accounting of the damage. Ben lay still, as if in a sarcophagus, while the machine banged and whirred and clanged its way to a picture of what had happened to his brain.

When your heart stops and blood does not move through your body to your brain, the areas that take it the hardest are the ones with the greatest need for oxygen and sugar—the parts of the brain that store our memories and control movement and learning. This was true in Ben's case; the MRI results revealed that his brain had not emerged unscathed. But he had been spared complete devastation, which meant that Andrea and Bryan could hope for some degree of recovery. The question was just how much.

Three days after Ben's body temperature rose to normal, he opened his eyes for the first time. It was a little step, but to his parents it was tremendous. Andrea had unlocked Ben's phone—easily, because her son had used the same two passwords since he was in the tenth grade—and when he opened his eyes that day, she sent out her first update to Ben's friends and family through his Facebook page: *"Ben opened his eyes this afternoon . . . Hopefully more tomorrow."* Andrea stayed glued to his bedside, hoping for the next step forward. Maybe there would be a purposeful movement, maybe even a word.

The minutes became hours and then days, one sliding into the next, vast stretches of nothingness punctuated by small but real victories. Ben opened his eyes a little bit more the next day, and when Andrea slid her hand into his, she felt the beginning of a squeeze. She updated his page with these details, too. But most of the time, there was little progress.

The window in Ben's hospital room faced the air-conditioning units of the neighboring building. Andrea remembers this view. She remembers the beeping of the machines. Ben's friends crowded the ICU waiting room and wrote goofy in-jokes on the "Get to know me" poster on the wall of Ben's hospital room. In between Andrea's upbeat updates, they posted to his Facebook feed with photos of a younger Ben—a chubby little brown-haired boy with a wide smile, a beaming teenager all dressed up with a date on his way to a school dance. Some days Ben would open his eyes and wince when one of the more forceful doctors pinched the bed of his toenail to test his level of consciousness and ability to respond to pain. Other days, he lay still.

Once he started to wake and intermittently respond to commands, Ben was no longer in what would be described as a vegetative state. He had passed into a new territory, this one termed a minimally conscious state. In early March, Andrea reported a sequence of *"good days"* on Facebook—first, Ben was able to keep his eyes open all day, and on another day, he laughed. The laugh was quieter than it had been. It was not that booming explosive laugh you could have heard from anywhere in the house, but it still felt like a clue to her that Ben was in there somewhere. But then, two days later, he was spiking high fevers from pneumonia, and doctors had to drain a liter of fluid that had collected around one of his lungs. They left a tube in his chest to collect the remaining fluid. *"He does not feel very good,"* Andrea wrote simply. *"Plan on short, quiet visits for now."*

The pneumonia improved. It felt like a move forward when he underwent the surgical procedures to place a tracheostomy tube and feeding tube. He couldn't yet speak, but with the breathing tube out of his mouth and instead hooked to the tracheostomy in his neck, he smiled and scowled in true Ben style. Weeks later, once he could breathe without the ventilator, Ben was finally able to move out of the ICU and into a regular room on the general medical floor. *"Ben graduated to a new room!"* Andrea announced on Facebook in mid-March. It was a single room, and Andrea promptly decorated it with pictures. There in that room, out of the intensive care unit, the pace of progress accelerated. Ben started to eat crackers and applesauce. His doctors switched out his tracheostomy tube for a smaller one, and then they were finally able to remove it altogether. Ben would later find the scar in his neck where the tube had been, and he would run his fingers curiously over the small patch of pink, raised skin. By late March, aspects of Ben's personality had started to return. He was alert enough to wink at his physical therapist and seemed to be flirting with his nurse.

Andrea tried to maintain her optimistic outlook. At first, the surge of adrenaline had numbed her worry. In those early hours and days, she had not been certain that her son would live, so she had simply been relieved at first when death did not come. It was all she could do to wake up, leave the house early enough to beat traffic on her way to the hospital, then spend the day sitting in her son's room, watching him and listening to the doctors and looking out the window until the sun set and the night nurses came. She liked to stay until after shift change, so

122

she could see who would be at her son's bedside all night and they could see her. But as the days wore on, a different fear crept in.

He was alive, but what was going to happen to him? After those initial days and weeks had passed, no one would tell her what to expect in the longer term or even offer her a range of possible outcomes with a best- and worst-case scenario. She watched Ben as she sat at his bedside. He could open his eyes and sometimes he could eat, but he still couldn't talk, and she wondered whether this would be it, if this was as far as they would ever get.

She understood that Ben's doctors were in a tough spot with these questions—they didn't want to limit hope, nor did they want to be unrealistic—but that didn't make the unknown any easier. "If I let myself think too much about what the future would be like..." Andrea paused. Her expression clouded, but only for a second. "I just couldn't go there." And so she did the only thing she could do. She continued to update Ben's page on Facebook. She encouraged those who were reading her updates to download and fill out a health-care proxy form, even if they were young, because you never know what might happen, and she wouldn't want anyone to have to struggle through the paperwork and waiting she had in order to become the guardian for her son (who'd never designated a proxy when he was healthy). And she focused on the next goal, which was leaving the hospital for the world that came after, that hopeful place called rehab.

Compared to the drab concrete of the hospital, the acute care rehab building actually sparkles. Though it is just minutes from the hospital where Ben had been taken after the overdose, and some of the same doctors work in both places, the rehab hospital looks like it is part of a different world. It is tall and new, and the walls are made of glass. You can see the Charles River from the patient rooms. It seems like the kind of place where something good can happen, and Andrea was excited to get there. Families generally are. Leaving the hospital means that the acute life-or-death catastrophe has passed, and it is time to begin picking up the pieces and start the task of getting better.

But there is anxiety in the move, too. Ben would not stay at rehab forever. With the transfer, the clock on acute inpatient rehabilitation benefits starts ticking (insurance companies might cover only six to ten weeks of inpatient rehab). That time frame forces families to confront the limits of what is possible and the fact that their loved one might not improve as much as they hope—not in the short term, and maybe not ever.

It had been a month since that Sunday morning when Ben's heart had stopped, and it was finally time to leave the hospital. The ambulance drove for about ten minutes before arriving at the modern building where Ben would spend the next few months. At the time, still among the ranks of the minimally conscious, Ben couldn't reliably follow instructions. But he could do things like reach for an object. He could eat. He could articulate words even though they didn't necessarily make sense, and this evidence of preserved language function landed him in a category of brain injury that is said to portend a better outcome. The day after he arrived at rehab, his mother wrote: *"The transition to the new place is slow. Ben sat in a wheelchair and we walked around the floor and checked out the views... Do not be alarmed if you come for a visit, Ben has a bed tent [a mesh cagelike enclosure around the bed] to keep him from trying to get out."*

Andrea missed only one day at rehab, for her daughter's musical. Her daughter was in her final year of high school, preparing to leave home for college. She and Andrea had both been looking forward to the time together, without her two brothers in the house. Things had changed—first Andrea's other son, Greg, moved home, and then Ben overdosed. Now Andrea could hardly keep track of which classes her daughter was taking that spring. Though she was no longer consumed by the daily fear that Ben would die, she didn't want to leave him alone. As if he were an infant again, she felt that she needed to be with him each day, to witness and to encourage and to be his voice when he could not speak for himself. She was there when, six weeks after his injury, Ben stood up from his wheelchair to take a step. On the same day, he brushed his own teeth. His mother watched him do that, too. *"Look out, here he comes!"* Andrea wrote.

"In full disclosure, I have been posting the best part

of Ben's days," Andrea wrote on Facebook a few weeks later. Ben had made his way out of minimal consciousness to "emerge" into conscious awareness, and he found this new world to be confusing and frustrating. Life was full of instructions he didn't know how to follow and objects and activities that felt familiar—despite his memory problems, Ben opened his phone without hesitation—but were somehow different. The doctors assured Andrea that Ben's agitation was normal, so she tried to interact calmly and to wait for the glimmers of recognition, for that Ben smile when he saw a friend, for his laugh or a hug.

One Monday afternoon a few weeks into Ben's rehab stay, a dozen clinicians gathered in a conference room on the seventh floor of the rehabilitation hospital to spend an hour talking about Ben's brain. This meeting takes place once a week, and the process is generally the same: one hour, one patient. The hour begins when neuropsychologist Joseph Giacino assumes his post at a round table in the middle of the room. His audience, ranging from physical therapists in scrubs and sneakers to neurologists in bow ties, sits in a semicircle against the wall, watching with interest while eating lunch. After relaying a brief history of the case, Dr. Giacino pulls up the patient's MRI on a large overhead monitor, scrolling through the pictures of the brain to display the extent of the damage. Stage set, he turns to the patient's doctors, nurses, and therapists to see if they have any questions for him. These will guide his exam.

Then the patient enters, often sitting in a wheelchair rolled in by a nurse. Dr. Giacino leans in as though he and the patient are the only two people in the room, and he begins to ask questions: What's your name? Do you know what happened to you? On other occasions, he will ask the patient to perform tasks, say, identifying all tokens of a specific color, remembering a list of objects, or reciting numbers backward. He will deconstruct the nuance of the response later. Each victory and each mistake means something, and the assembled audience watches in rapt attention.

By the time it was Ben's turn to be examined in this clinic, he had fully emerged into the world of consciousness, and he could walk with a walker and he could speak, but his therapists had noticed a problem with what Dr. Giacino described to me as a suppressed drive. If you asked Ben a question, he'd answer and do what you told him, but he didn't initiate conversation or action. Left alone, he was rather still and silent. When he did speak, his voice was so soft that it was almost inaudible, termed "hypophonic." Sometimes, when he walked with his physical therapist down the rehab building's long halls, his regular strides would break into tiny little steps up on his tiptoes. This is what's called a "festinating" gait (from the Latin "to hurry"). When Ben wrote, he started out with normal-sized letters, but these quickly degenerated into tiny, cramped chicken scratch, or "micrographia."

This constellation—hypophonia, festinating gait, micrographia—is actually characteristic of Parkinson's disease, and this is what the team wanted to talk about at the weekly meeting. It wasn't that Ben had developed Parkinson's after his brain injury. Ben could actually snap out of the behaviors if someone specifically told him to speak up or to take larger steps. And so it seemed that these problems were all related to the damage to Ben's drive and motor control that had been caused by his brain injury. Maybe stimulants would help, but on the other hand, too much nonspecific stimulation might make these problems worse. There was no easy answer, no drug or device that could resolve Ben's tiny steps or make him speak louder or return him to himself again. There's rarely a simple answer here in the Monday clinic. Brain injuries are messy. The relationship between damage, behavior, and the possibility of recovery is not always so clear. As a result, Ben's hour concluded with the best plan possible, given these limitations: hopefully, if enough people corrected Ben, in a standardized manner, he would be able to recognize and in time learn to change these behaviors on his own.

With that goal in mind, the physical therapists continued to work with Ben, taking pains to point out to him when he slipped into these patterns. By the end of May he could walk with minimal assistance, although he still needed prompting, and he could talk and eat nearly anything he wanted on his own. His physical therapists took him out on the Charles River in a boat, perhaps to show his family that even if he was not the same, he could still do things he'd once enjoyed. In general, the next step at this point would have been to transfer Ben to another rehabilitation facility, located up in the mountains of New Hampshire.

But when it came time for another transfer, Andrea and her husband were conflicted. They wanted Ben to make the most progress he could during that first year after his injury, when it's said the bulk of recovery takes place, and already three months had gone by. Yes, he could walk and talk and eat, but he was still so far from the person he had been before the overdose. Maybe he would never get there. But Andrea and Bryan weren't certain that another rehab, far from home, would be the best place for him. Neither driving up to New Hampshire every day nor moving there seemed to make all that much sense. It had been too long, and they just wanted their son with them. So they began to make plans to bring Ben back home.

Andrea holds a master's in religious education, and she thought she would go back to work once her daughter left home for college in the fall, but that would wait. Motherhood took center stage once again. She wouldn't take care of everything—Ben was a twenty-four-year-old man, after all, so an aide would come to help him get into the shower and a nurse would check his vital signs. She coordinated a small army of nurses and therapists—physical, occupational, and speech—who would come to the house to monitor Ben's health and help him regain as much independence as he could. An exercise room on the first floor became Ben's room, his bed equipped with an alarm that would go off if he got up in the middle of the night. And just a little more than three months after his overdose, on the day before his sister's high school graduation, Ben came home.

Ben had been home about a month. As Andrea told me her son's story, from the drugs to the cardiac arrest to the brain injury, Ben sat with us at the kitchen table, dogs lazing idly at our feet. I felt uncomfortable at first, talking about Ben with Ben beside me, although he didn't seem to be listening and surely didn't seem to mind, even when his mother described how close he had come to dying. He was there, a solid physical presence, but it wasn't really clear how much of the whole thing he could understand. He didn't remember the injury or much of the year that preceded it, so it seemed to Andrea that his mind had tried to fill in the blanks with the data he had. After seeing so many patients with shaved heads and scars on their skulls while he was at inpatient rehab, he'd decided that he must have been in a car accident, or maybe he had been shot. Every time someone told him what had actually happened, it seemed like the first time he'd heard the news.

But memories from high school and college lingered.

"What did you play?" Andrea asked Ben of his years in high school sports.

He spoke quietly but clearly. "Football..."

"Do you remember anything else you played?" Andrea probed.

He scrunched up his face as though he were digging through a storage facility for that album he knew must be there somewhere.

Andrea gave him a clue. "You went to the mountain?"

He thought a bit longer.

"Snowboarding team," he replied. I felt relieved, and stifled my inclination to exclaim, "Good job!"

Perhaps Ben did not know what had happened to him, but I wondered if he knew that his life was different, that he could no longer call his friends to plan a trip or grab the keys and leave the house in a huff. Ben and his brother, Greg, had always made each other laugh, and sometimes they still could. They'd cracked up over something silly in the back of the car the other day, and it felt as though a bit more of Ben had emerged again, and that was great. But most of Ben's friends, even the ones who had been the most attentive when he was in the hospital, had stopped coming by as they returned to their new jobs and apartments. Some still visited occasionally, but it was hard, because even if Ben enjoyed spending time in their company, it wasn't obvious. He wasn't the one to initiate conversations or make plans.

I wondered if on some level he was saddened by all this loss, even if it was beyond his ability to articulate the feeling. Andrea thought about this, too. When Ben said he didn't want to go out to a place where she knew his friends might be or shook his head when she asked him to bring his wheelchair into a store, she wondered whether he felt self-conscious. It was hard to tell. It seemed equally possible that the Ben who sat in front of me that day felt himself to be the only Ben Clancy that had ever existed.

"Do you feel like you're the same as you were before?" Andrea asked.

"Yeah…," Ben responded.

"Do you feel like anything is different?"

A shrug. "Not really."

Andrea kept her eyes on her son. "I think that you're a lot quieter." She turned to me. "Ben had this loud voice and laugh, and it was always going. It's still there, I think, but the volume is turned down."

As we talked, the three dogs raced to the back door, barking as Ben's occupational therapist stood outside. Since his return home she had been working with Ben on some skills, such as assembling ingredients and preparing a sandwich, and getting into the bathroom to sit down on the shower chair. Ben was "the sandwich man" before the brain injury, Andrea told me. It didn't matter if it was ten in the morning or late at night: Ben was notorious for concocting some kind of delicious masterpiece and eating it with gusto. It was no surprise to Andrea that he would still be able to make a sandwich after his injury.

On that day the physical therapist was on break, so

the occupational therapist had decided to do some PT exercises with Ben. She passed him purple three-pound weights and placed her hand on the small of his back as he lifted his arms up and down ten times. Before the overdose, Ben would have balked if someone had handed him weights that were so small and purple and unequivocally feminine, but it was the most that he could lift with his balance and coordination the way they were. Moving on to the legs, they stood against the kitchen counter and Ben lifted his leg from side to side, over and over again. His mother channeled one of his high school coaches to encourage him: "C'mon, Clancy!" Ben's lips rose in a slight smile, but he remained silent.

It was time to practice walking. Ben had scared his mother a week or so before, when she had left him alone in the kitchen for a few minutes and returned to find him gone. He had gotten out of his wheelchair, stood up, and walked up the stairs to the second floor. He was fine, but she knew that was just luck. He could have been hurt. She wondered what might happen if he wandered outside and someone saw his unsteady gait, assumed that he was drunk, called the police, and Ben didn't know how to respond. "You imagine horrible things," she told me.

To help mitigate her concerns, she bought Ben a red ID bracelet bearing his name, address, and information about his brain injury. He'd grown deeply confused the first time he started wearing it, insisting he needed to put on his bracelet even though it was already there on his wrist, exactly where it was supposed to be. Andrea tried to explain, pointing to his wrist to show him he already had the ID bracelet on and that everything was okay, but he couldn't seem to put those facts together. She watched him grow more frustrated until he simply stopped trying to understand, bewildered and deflated. "For him to give up, that's just not like him." Andrea sighed. "He was a great arguer."

Ben walked slowly down the hall. The occupational therapist grabbed the back of his belt when it seemed he might pitch over. His gait briefly degenerated into the tiny tiptoe steps Dr. Giacino had described, but the therapist reminded him to take "big steps, Ben," and the walk normalized. When he came back down the hall, Ben struggled to get his feet in the right position to ease himself into his wheelchair. The tasks of turning around a corner and walking backward seemed particularly challenging, and we watched for a few long seconds before Ben allowed his body to sink comfortably back into the chair.

With Ben in his chair, the session was over. That was it—forty-five minutes. Later in the day, the speech therapist would stop by. In between, there would be a sandwich to make and some television and some rest, but time was passing quickly, and it was hard to measure many day-to-day gains. With physical, occupational, and speech therapy sessions occurring only twice a week, so much of Ben's potential for recovery seemed to ride on all the other minutes of the day when Andrea and Ben were alone. Sometimes it went smoothly, and they read together or played games and Ben did his PT exercises, but other days he wasn't in the mood, and it was hard for Andrea to force her twenty-four-year-old son to stay motivated to regain the independence she wasn't sure he was even aware of having lost. While it was easy to let a day go by with little to show for it, the weeks were turning into months. Andrea and Bryan sometimes feared they had made a mistake by choosing to bring Ben back home and that his potential for progress might be waning.

They had started looking into day programs near their home where Ben could receive therapy in a more structured fashion. They were particularly excited about one such facility, where Ben could get physical therapy in a gym and work on speaking more audibly and remembering what he had done the day before. The rehab had a pool and a yoga room, and there was even a little market where Ben could practice going to the store and buying things. Once or twice a week there would be an extra activity in the afternoon, perhaps a lawn game or a swim or mini-golf. Because it was a rehab for people with brain injuries, most of the other patients would inevitably be stroke survivors who were far older than Ben, but occasionally there might be someone closer to his age.

Ben had taken a tour, and at the time he seemed to like the place. He even remembered a few details about it the next day, although he hadn't been able to recall them since. And so Andrea and Bryan were optimistic, "pinning a lot of hopes" on the possibility. Was it the best in the world of options? Andrea didn't know. There was no way to know, really. The clear protocols that had guided Ben's initial days and weeks had been replaced by the feeling that they were flying blind. But Andrea did know that Ben would be busy there, and that having a place to go during the day would be good for him. And maybe someone could tap into his competitive spirit and motivate him in a way that Andrea, on her own, could not.

Andrea likes to plan, and in a way it seems that looking forward and thinking about what might come next saves her. She had started to fill out the paperwork that could allow Ben an aide who would come to the home for a few hours a couple of times each week. Andrea worried that Ben would view the aide as a babysitter—he wouldn't stand for that, and that wasn't what Andrea wanted—but it would help if there were someone else around so that she could get out of the house to run a few errands. And then, maybe in a few months, Ben would be able to undergo some structured cognitive testing, just to see where he was. There was a lot swirling about, and Andrea knew it. It could be overwhelming, but she needed the momentum. "If we stopped . . . I guess I just don't want to stop," she said. "I don't want to reach the point where we're not going forward anymore."

For the time being, Ben and his mother would continue to spend nearly every waking hour together. Before the brain injury, they'd been "like gas and a match." Ben could be a funny, loving guy, but he had a temper, too, and mother and son set each other off unlike anyone else. Whether Ben was arguing a contrarian political view to get a rise out of someone, or announcing his plans to go out against his parents' wishes, when Ben was there, you knew it. Now, in a way, being with Ben was simple. "There's no drama, there's no arguing or disagreements. That part, it's nice," Andrea said. Some friends and relatives seemed to feel that their job was to keep Ben talking, quizzing him on the past and asking him questions, but not so for Andrea. She knew things could be far worse. When Ben was at rehab, she had seen parents caring for adult children who would likely spend the rest of their lives institutionalized, unable to walk or talk or eat on their own again. Ben was home and it was easy to be with him, and their quiet moments together were tender and good.

But still she missed her son, that charismatic young man who felt so deeply, whose curiosity led him to pore through Reuters news online each day, who made her furious but could also make her laugh in a way no one else could. It is a strange thing to miss someone while he is sitting next to you, maybe even to mourn him a little bit. "I'd love to be able to have the kind of interesting conversations we had in the past," Andrea told me. "I look at him sometimes and I think, *What is it going to be? Are*

we going to get there? Are we going to have conversa-
tions and interactions that aren't just, Do you want a
drink of water?"

These are questions that will be answered in time,
maybe in a year or two, or maybe even longer. In five years,
both of Ben's younger siblings will likely be out of the
house, living their own lives, and Ben will be nearing thirty.
Maybe he'll have his own apartment, with a job to go to
during the day, or maybe he will have made it out of the
house to live in a supervised setting. But perhaps he will be
living at home still, with his mother, in his room on the first
floor.

Ben's heart had stopped. He would have died, but modern medicine had intervened to start his heart again. Doctors had cooled his body until it was freezing, and then they
warmed his body back up. Now he was home in shorts,
a T-shirt, and sneakers, sitting at his kitchen table. With
all the uncertainty ahead, there was the summer day, and
the present; lunchtime, and Ben was going to make a sandwich. Andrea took the ingredients out of the fridge. She
offered Ben turkey or prosciutto, cheese, lettuce, mustard,
and then the choice of a roll or sliced bread. She held up
the two types of bread, and Ben, the sandwich man, wordlessly reached out and chose the roll. He split it, slowly laid
out the turkey slices, layered on the cheese, and topped it
off with a squeeze of mustard. The dogs sat at his feet, as if
hoping for a bit of meat to fall from the table. The kitchen
was quiet.

* * *

One afternoon about a month after I first met Ben Clancy and his mother, I observed Ben's outpatient therapy at the rehab hospital near his home. Ben hadn't been going there long, and there weren't any patients his age after all, but Andrea was feeling good about her choice. Watching Ben in the gym that day working on balance and coordination with his physical therapist, I was struck by how far his physical abilities had progressed in just those few weeks. He was able to balance and turn and walk in ways that clearly would have thrown him off the day I had first met him, back in his home. I noted that to Andrea, and she seemed happy to hear my take. She knew Ben had been doing well, but she was with him every moment, so progress was harder for her to see. Ben smiled, too, but he was still quiet, and in a way passive.

He struggled with memory, and his therapists had equipped him with a binder so that he could record his activities and what he ate each day. On the day I observed him, Ben's occupational therapist took him to the kitchen. He didn't seem as interested in food as he'd been before the accident, and he kept losing weight. So that afternoon Ben was going to practice making a grilled cheese sandwich. He stood at the stove, waiting for a prompt from the therapist. As I watched him carefully following the instructions, I thought again of that boisterous Ben I had never met, who would whip himself up something delicious regardless of the hour. Ben hesitated and left one side of the sandwich on the stove for too long. The small room filled with a not-unpleasant smell of burnt toast and cheese. The therapist coached him to scrape the burnt and blackened piece of bread off the cheese so he could salvage a good half sandwich. He placed it on a plate and sat down. We all watched as he took a few bites.

6

Where the Bridge Ends

I noticed the scars when we met. Not in the first moments, when all I felt was the energy of this pretty woman around my own age and her husband, a police officer with an affable demeanor and strong handshake. But then as we sat and talked I registered the healed wounds where the tubes had entered her neck, the tracheostomy tube first and then the garden hose of a catheter that had carried blood out of her jugular vein and through a machine next to her hospital bed.

I didn't see the rest of the scars until Cindy Scribner lifted her shirt, surprising me mid-conversation to show me her abdomen. That was where surgeons had opened and closed her when she was bleeding inside. The pale skin there was jagged where the edges met, as though it had been violated too many times. Her chest and belly were studded with evidence of other invasions—a collapsed lung, another bleed. A final thin scar ran under her breasts where her chest had been cut open like the shell of a clam so that surgeons could replace her lungs with a pair taken from an even younger woman who had died.

In telling Cindy's story, I find myself wondering where to begin. In a way, the story starts with a machine. That's how I came to meet Cindy, after all—because of the lung bypass that had kept her from dying while she waited for a transplant. Of all the technologies in the hospital, I found this one particularly compelling. Even the name, extracorporeal membrane oxygenation, or ECMO, struck me as futuristic, like a science fiction trope that has become reality.

On this machine you can watch your blood exit your body through large catheters, turn from dark blue to oxygenated red, and return to your body again, multiple times every minute. You are alive and awake, but that life is so precarious you can't leave the ICU. So you wait days and weeks and even months for a transplant or for your lungs to recover, all the while fearing a complication. "In the scope of what we do to humans, this is the kitchen sink," one surgeon told me.

Though it's currently at the cutting edge, I'm told that ECMO will become standard practice in intensive care units in a matter of years. And I wanted to know the details. For example, how does someone who is awake on ECMO pass the hours? When days become weeks, does it begin to feel like life, or is each day just a counting down of the time in purgatory? And what if you are waiting for a transplant but it doesn't come? Is it possible to live indefinitely in an intensive care unit? And if it isn't, well, what then?

Because those questions are what brought me to Cindy, I could start with her in a hospital gown; her husband, Derek, flipping through TV channels trying to mask his fear; thick catheters and tubing; a machine that chatters and clangs. But maybe I should start when the symptoms did, nearly a decade earlier, when Cindy began to cough.

I imagine her, a young nurse at the time, married with two children already and another on the way. Likely she was so busy with her growing family that she paid little attention to the dry cough that came on like a tickle in her throat. At first it was just an annoyance. But when the cough started to keep her up at night and she coughed so hard in the morning before work that she'd gag and retch, she managed to fit in a visit to her doctor. He prescribed her an inhaler and considered ordering a chest X-ray if that didn't help, but it didn't seem worth the risk to Cindy's pregnancy. It was just a cough. One of her friends suggested the unlikely theory that her cough was somehow related to pregnancy and it would remit as mysteriously as it had appeared after she gave birth. She hoped so.

But the baby was born and she kept coughing. At that point it had been going on for months, so her doctor decided she should get the chest X-ray after all. A day or so later, Cindy's phone rang. She grabbed it, probably distracted as she juggled the phone, the infant on her hip, and the two young daughters clamoring for her attention. I can imagine how her body tensed and her daughters' high-pitched excitement faded into the background as she took in her doctor's sober tone: "Cindy. The radiologists are telling me there's something wrong. You need to see a pulmonologist."

She tried to stay calm through it all, even when the specialist explained to her how he would put her to sleep and pass a small flexible tube with a camera at the end of it down her throat, through her trachea, to take a sample of her lungs. Everything looked normal, he told her afterward, and though she kept coughing, she must have repeated these words to herself as evidence that she was fine, that everything could go back to the way it was before, that it would all be okay.

Cindy coughed through another pregnancy and the birth of her fourth girl. Sometimes when she ran after her daughters she was struck by an odd awareness of her ragged breath and pounding heart, but she managed to keep her fears tucked away in the background—until one morning, when she stood up and it was as if there wasn't enough air in the room. She was at work at the time, so she grabbed an oxygen probe and stuck it on her finger, and in that surreal moment she watched the number sink. Hands trembling, she called her doctor, who set things in motion to send her from the local hospital to Boston for more tests that led, finally, to a diagnosis: idiopathic pulmonary fibrosis, commonly referred to as IPF, a scarring of the lungs without a known cause.

It's not cancer but might as well be. Sitting in the office of the Boston specialist, Derek and Cindy heard the words, but it must have been nearly impossible to wrap their minds around the meaning. There's no cure; half of the people with this disease die within five years, and, implausibly, the only treatment that might prolong Cindy's life would be a lung transplant. Cindy had never even heard of this thing, and yet a doctor was telling her that it might kill her. She had lost her parents when she was young, remembered bouncing from relative to relative and home to home, and knew that she would do anything to protect her daughters from such an unsettled childhood. So when her doctor mentioned transplant, as scared as she was and as far-fetched as that hope sounded, she grabbed on to it and she did not let go.

Do I start the story there, the day everything changed?

Or does it start in a hospital room with Cindy hooked to a machine that would save her life if it did not destroy it? Maybe it begins later still, the day her surgeons gave her newly transplanted lungs. Any starting point is ultimately arbitrary, yet it frames what the story becomes. And Cindy's story is not just about ECMO, as I had thought it would be, or about being a mother with a fatal lung disease, or even about what it is like to live with the bittersweet gift of a lung transplant.

So instead, I'll tell Cindy's story the way she chose to show it to me the day we met.

* * *

The first real scar, the one in the middle of Cindy's neck, just below the spot where her vocal cords sit, is from the tracheostomy tube.

After the shock of the diagnosis, time did not speed, as Cindy might have thought it would. It moved along at a plodding pace, weeks and then months fading one into another with the sameness of doctor visits, tests, and waiting. Derek tried to keep the tone light by finding ways to joke, even when Cindy's doctors determined that she needed to carry oxygen with her during the day, and Cindy offered a smiling approximation of her prior self in return, but she hated the way life had shifted. Though she wanted to stay positive, she dreaded the curious stares that followed her as she walked down the street with her portable oxygen tank and four children in tow. She didn't want to scare her girls with the medical equipment, and she didn't want to have to ask for help to do simple things like cleaning the house or doing the dishes or playing with her daughters.

And then there was the waiting. First there was the wait to get on the transplant list, and even after she'd made it through the office visits that felt like interviews and endured test after laborious test, there was the wait for a call that wouldn't come. The transplant wait times in the Boston area are notoriously long, and Cindy's blood type was hard to match. As months and then years passed, and Cindy became more easily winded, tethered not just by the oxygen tubing but also by her worsening lung function, she worried that this was it. She didn't sit by the phone. Her heart didn't jump each time it rang. Deep down, she didn't expect that a transplant would ever come.

Keenly aware that her health would only decline over time, Cindy resolved to stay as active in her family's life as she could. So one Mother's Day, a few years after her diagnosis, Cindy dragged her tired body to a field near her home to watch one of her daughters play in a flag football game. Though her head throbbed, she waited until after the game to tell Derek how her mind felt foggy and all she wanted to do was fall asleep. The cough and breathlessness had grown familiar to her by now, but this was different, she explained. Something wasn't right. Unable to shake their mounting worry, Derek and Cindy drove the familiar hour from their home, just over the Massachusetts–New Hampshire border, down to Boston. It was already late when they got to the ER, and it was going to take hours to get Cindy a bed on the general medical floor. As the time crept on, she encouraged Derek to go home. She'd be okay.

Cindy doesn't remember this part, but at some point after Derek left she stopped breathing. The doctors rushed to her and when they could not rouse her, they moved to intubate. They called Derek on his cell and he turned his car around—he was lucky he didn't get into an accident—to speed back to the hospital. This, Derek remembers, was the moment "when hell began."

He learned that the carbon dioxide levels in Cindy's blood had been climbing, which explained her headache and fuzzy feeling earlier in the day. When they reached dangerous levels there in the ER, her breathing slowed and then halted completely. The tempo shifted; the last bits of normalcy eroded. Up in the ICU, Cindy's doctors spent days trying to get her to breathe on her own, but with her degree of fibrosis, her lungs were too damaged. So they brought Derek the consent form for a tracheostomy tube. He scrawled his name almost without thinking, because he was in Boston and he was scared but he trusted the doctors and wanted them to do whatever they could to save his wife's life. If it were up to him, they wouldn't even ask.

After the tracheotomy, Cindy woke slowly. At first, still trapped inside the swirling delirium of her mind, she saw babies crying on her bed, imagined rain coming from the ceiling, and believed that her husband had cheated on her with the nurses. When the meds started to clear, she found herself in a different sort of nightmare. She opened her mouth but made no sound. There was a tube in her neck connecting her to the ventilator, and slowly she pieced it all together; she had taken care of patients with tracheostomy tubes, and now, while she'd been unconscious, she had become one of them. Unable to talk, too weak even to write, Cindy was "heartbroken" and maybe even a little angry with Derek because he had given the okay for this to happen to her. But she didn't tell him that. She knew him well enough to know that under his police officer's controlled exterior, he was in over his head. They both were. Besides, he hadn't been offered any acceptable alternatives. So she kept her thoughts to herself. And she waited.

Waiting sounds static, safe, almost. But really, it was as if she were balanced on a tightrope: the smallest perturbation could mean disaster. And while she waited, just as Derek and the kids were getting ready for her to come back home, though now with a trach and a ventilator, Cindy spiked a fever. Her oxygen needs skyrocketed. Back in the intensive care unit, doctors gathered around Cindy's bed, their movements crisp and language sparse, stripped of the casual jokes that so often pepper conversation. Derek paced the windowless hallway outside the ICU for minutes that felt like hours, so nervous he was almost vibrating, until one of the doctors, Phillip Camp, emerged to talk with him. Camp is a burly man who's both a transplant surgeon and a lieutenant colonel in the U.S. Air Force, and he has the reassuring, unwavering confidence of someone who has actually seen it all. I imagine him leading Derek to a small conference room, the type with plastic chairs and a table sticky with pastries other families had nibbled on the worst days of their lives, to tell him about something called ECMO.

Even with the ventilator at its highest settings, Cindy's oxygen levels were teetering. So Dr. Camp explained that if Derek gave the okay, he would place two catheters in Cindy's largest veins, one in her neck and one in her groin.

Cindy's blood would leave her body through one of these catheters and run through a machine next to her bed. After the machine had done its job, which was to take the place of Cindy's lungs, the healthy blood would return to her body through the other catheter. The surgeon told Derek that once his wife was connected to this machine, she might not need the ventilator any longer, so she could wake up and maybe even talk. If things went well, the surgeons would replace the catheter in her groin with a single two-part catheter in her neck. With her legs free, Cindy would be able, and required, to walk. This was important, Derek would learn. Walking would be necessary if she was going to stay strong enough to remain on the lung transplant waiting list.

Sometimes it's hard to decide whether to start ECMO—if it seems too early in the course of illness, maybe it's not worth the risk; if it seems too late, the patient might already be too far gone. With few strict rules to govern this decision, it's a difficult judgment when someone is on the border of being too old or too sick with other diseases to benefit. But for the team taking care of Cindy, the decision was about as clear as it gets. Already, she'd been on the list for lung transplant, which meant that a group of doctors had methodically considered her case and deemed her body and mind able to withstand one of medicine's most aggressive interventions. Besides, Dr. Camp knew Cindy. He had seen her in outpatient appointments, he had been the one to take her to the OR when she needed the tracheostomy tube, and he knew she was stubborn and "exquisitely focused" on doing whatever she had to do to stay alive for her children.

When Camp talks to families about starting a loved one on ECMO, and about the lines and tubes and repeated bronchoscopies that come with it, he knows he is talking to men and women in the midst of incomprehensible crisis who might not remember much of what he says. He is honest in these conversations, but he is gentle, too, as he lays the groundwork for what might come.

A patient whose life is being prolonged by this machine can bleed or she can clot. Either of these outcomes can be devastating and possibly fatal. And unlike the VAD for the heart or dialysis for the kidneys, ECMO isn't designed to support the failing lungs indefinitely. Think of ECMO as a bridge, Camp explains. A bridge goes from one place to another. That means the bridge has to end somewhere, either at recovery or at transplant. So if at some point things aren't going the way everyone hopes, and those goals are no longer achievable, Dr. Camp and his team might decide that ECMO needs to stop.

But at the moment, one fact was clear: Cindy's doctors needed to do something. Her small ICU room was transformed into a makeshift OR. Operating room nurses arrived bearing sterile surgical trays and headlamps. There was barely enough space for all the people and their equipment, and from outside the room it must have looked like chaos, but once Dr. Camp prepped Cindy's groin and neck and made the first incisions, time slowed. He felt the room go quiet as his concentration intensified. He didn't know if Cindy would live to make it to transplant, but he did know that if all went as well as it possibly could, ECMO would buy Cindy something she didn't have otherwise—time to wait for lungs.

Days later, Cindy awoke to a new constellation of horrors. She was scared to move her head, worried that she would dislodge the ECMO catheter in her neck and die while her blood cascaded from the tubing. Though she didn't want to move, she soon learned that if she didn't get up and walk, if she let herself be paralyzed by panic, she could be taken off the transplant list.

Just lifting her head was a struggle; I can't imagine the effort it must have taken to stand. But even though she was tired and in pain and scared, she placed one foot in front of the other, with nurses and physical therapists behind and in front to make sure she didn't fall and injure herself or the machine that was keeping her alive. On the few days when she felt that it was all too much, Dr. Camp would come to her room and stand at the foot of her bed and tell her that she had a choice: "Either you get yourself up, or I'm going to have to make you." It wasn't just a walk. He knew the stakes. One day would slide into the next, and if she didn't get out of bed and grew too weak to tolerate a transplant, or ended up with a complication, the transplant team would have to take her off the list and it would all be over. So it was a walk or "a drag," he told her, and she would walk just to spite him. That daily walk was the price she paid for the uncertain hope of freedom.

She held on to bits of routine. In the morning, if she felt good, Cindy applied mascara and eye shadow while the news played in the background. Her nurses washed her hair. The guys at work had all donated their sick time to Derek, so he spent each day in the hospital, with walks to Dunkin' Donuts across the street for a break if Cindy was feeling good enough for an iced coffee. During the day and into the evening, other family members stopped by. Her youngest child was terrified at first and would sit on Cindy's sister's lap for comfort rather than approach her mother in the hospital bed. In the afternoon, another relative or friend would drive the older kids over. They'd do their homework and watch television. Sometimes Derek blew air into the hospital gloves to turn them into balloons that the girls could bat around the room. There were lots of food deliveries, maybe frozen yogurt one night, Olive Garden another. When everyone had left and it was Cindy and Derek alone again, they'd turn on a movie and try to concentrate. Derek would sit in a chair at the bedside, and he'd wait there until Cindy fell asleep. Then he'd slip out, careful not to wake her, to close his eyes for a few hours or to go to the bar near the hospital for a couple of beers to calm his nerves.

As Cindy's weeks in the ICU became months, the carefully cultivated distance that keeps us doctors from our patients began to disappear. There were little things, like the time one of the doctors went to Walmart late at night to buy Cindy a huge water gun so she could surprise Dr. Camp when he came by on rounds. Or the way a resident burst into tears when she saw Cindy's youngest child jump onto her hospital stretcher, so excited to see her mother that she no longer seemed to notice the lines and tubes and blood. Or the time the anesthesiologist on the ECMO team surprised Derek with a room at a fancy hotel in downtown Boston, just to give him a break from night after night curled up on a couch in the ICU family waiting room.

But what Cindy's doctors could not get for her was what she needed most—a set of lungs. And after weeks on ECMO, Cindy started to bleed. First she bled into her abdomen. It took the surgeons a long time in the OR to control the bleeding, and then, because she was still on blood thinners to tolerate ECMO, she bled into her chest. Again and again, blood accumulated around her lungs, necessitating trips to the OR to open the chest, drain the blood, and look for the source. She would return upstairs to her ICU bed sedated, and when she woke she'd find herself in pain, her body swollen from the fluids she'd received in the OR. Each time, she was determined to get up and start walking as quickly as she could. But a few days later, she'd start bleeding from somewhere else.

Cindy and Derek didn't talk about the possibility that a transplant might not come in time, but as each day passed and the complications became more frequent, they couldn't help but think it. When Cindy had fallen asleep at night, Derek lay awake in the family room. He made promises. If Cindy got a transplant and she lived, he'd be the perfect husband. He'd never get annoyed. He'd be endlessly patient. When a doctor or nurse entered the family room in the night, he'd feel as if his heart had stopped, and he would wait there, unmoving, terrified that something had happened to his wife. Only when the footsteps veered away from the couch where he slept and toward someone else could he start breathing again.

Cindy asked anyone who happened to be in her hospital room whether she would make it. She didn't want to talk about her fears or engage in a conversation about the possibility that she might not get lungs. She just wanted someone to tell her that she would be okay. So the doctor or nurse or even the family member who heard her request would give her the response she was looking for: "Cindy, you're going to get there." She'd nod, trying to make herself believe the words, and for a second she would feel safe. But alone with her thoughts, Cindy couldn't shake the fear that the lungs would never come and that she would never again see her children outside that hospital room.

Derek could tell that Cindy, despite her insistence on continuing to walk and put on her makeup and see her children, was growing weaker. He knew she kept bleeding, and each time she went down to the OR she'd come back up with more tubes and drains attached to her. Though he never admitted his fears to Cindy, he started to suspect that they were near the end, and in spite of himself he began to think about the fact that he might lose his wife. He would sell the house they'd bought together, he figured. He'd move with the kids to a town closer to his work so he could see them during the day. But if he followed that train of thought any further, his chest got tight and he couldn't breathe, as if he were about to have a heart attack.

Even the unfailingly optimistic thoracic surgeon, Dr. Camp, began to wonder whether Cindy was reaching the end of the bridge and if it was time to shift the course they had set out on so many weeks before. He could make more trips to the OR, find something to patch, and then cross his fingers until she bled again. But he felt increasingly uncertain that this was in Cindy's best interest. "You see the pain you're causing her, and you have this horrible dilemma, wondering if you have changed from doing this *for* somebody to doing this *to* somebody," Dr. Camp told me. "I was starting to worry that we had come up to that line."

Shifting course would mean acknowledging the very real possibility that Cindy would not get lungs. It might mean deciding not to return to the OR the next time Cindy bled, focusing instead on treating her pain and her fear. Ultimately, it might mean stopping ECMO.

I've removed a breathing tube from a person who will die without it, and I have stood just outside the room, looking at my feet as I waited for the last slow breaths to stop and the monitor to go flat. But in these cases the person has been unaware and death has been imminent, unavoidable with or without the tube. With ECMO, we are talking about something different. We are talking about removing a life-prolonging machine that is no longer serving its purpose from someone who is awake and able to interact with the world, knowing that without it, that person will die.

Dr. Camp's team had taken care of Cindy in the hospital for more than two months. They'd seen her and Derek and the children every day and they had become close, maybe too close, but that's where they were. "If you're too far away, you sometimes don't appreciate why you should go the extra mile for a patient," Dr. Camp reflected. "But if you're too close, you might not see why you should stop."

Just before sunrise the day before Halloween, Dr. Camp was still at home when he got the page. Cindy was bleeding again. He rushed back to the hospital to examine her and to make a plan. There in the intensive care unit where Cindy had lived for more than seventy days, he and his colleagues considered their options. He could take her back to the OR. He could open her chest and stanch the bleeding, knowing that it would start again. Or he could explain to Cindy and Derek that they had come up against the limits of what was possible, and this was the time to stop. With some hesitation, early that morning Camp booked an OR.

He called Derek to let him know that he would take Cindy back down to try to stop the bleeding. It might be the last time.

Soon after he made plans with the OR, his pager went off. Lungs. It had happened to him before, this sort of eleventh-hour notification just when it seemed the tides had turned against his patient. He logged on to his computer and started digging through the available information. The lungs looked good. He called his team. The next call went to Derek's cell phone. Derek was on the way to the hospital anyway, but he recognized the number and picked up quickly.

"I have some news for you," Camp said.

"What?" Derek replied, anxious. "How's Cindy?"

"We're going to take her to the OR, but for something different."

"Is it going to help her?" Derek asked.

"I think so," the surgeon said. "We're going to put some lungs in her."

Derek lost it. He was still driving, so Camp told him to pull over. On the side of the road, he collected himself. He had heard something different in the surgeon's voice earlier that morning when he told him about the plans for the OR, a certain muted tone where before there had been optimism. But now, after everything, Cindy might get lungs. Derek drove to his aunt's house and told her the news. Then he called Camp back. He wanted to make sure this was for real. "How certain is it?" Derek asked. "I wouldn't be calling you if I didn't think these were the ones," the surgeon replied.

When the doctors told Cindy that her trip to the operating room was postponed and that she would be getting her transplant later that night, she didn't know how to react. She knew that she should feel overjoyed, but she was tired and she was in pain, and honestly, all she wanted was for someone to tell her that she would be okay. Her doctors reassured her, and then they asked an unexpected question. "What do you like to drink?" Cindy had never had much of a taste for alcohol, even before she got sick. But she did like a good margarita.

The team would be awake in the OR all night, and so before the case started, Dr. Camp and David Silver, the anesthesiologist on the team, went out to dinner at the TGI Fridays across the street from the hospital. The doctors knew that the transplant would be risky; with all the bleeding and the prior surgeries, there was a real chance that Cindy would not live. No one should miss a chance to celebrate a transplant, and so they would bring Cindy a celebratory drink beforehand. Fridays serves great big margaritas, the kind that make you feel like you're at the beach. As it turns out, you can't order a margarita to go, at least not from Fridays, so the doctors settled on virgin margarita mix, and then they swung by the liquor store to get Cindy a few small bottles of tequila. They brought the ingredients up to her hospital room in a brown paper bag. There, before her transplant, they opened one of the bottles and poured the smooth amber liquor into the margarita mix. Cindy, with the anesthesiologist's blessing, took a sip. Derek pulled out his phone and took a photo of that moment, his wife in the hospital bed on the eve of her transplant, catheters sticking out of her neck, smiling hesitantly with a brown paper bag and a Styrofoam cup.

When it came time to take Cindy down to the OR, Dr. Silver promised Derek that he would keep him updated. Cindy managed a joke for the doctors before they put her under—maybe they could do a quick breast augmentation while they were in there? It was dark by then. Derek lay back down on the couch in the family room where he had spent so many nights, waking every hour, panicked and wondering if he had missed a call. In the OR, the surgeon who opened Cindy's chest with a horizontal incision under her breasts worked to clear the blood obstructing his view.

Early on Halloween morning Derek woke to a call. The first lung was in, and the surgeons were starting on the second. This would be the final scar.

While she was in the hospital, Cindy was transfused over 160 pints of blood. That is more than sixteen times the amount of blood in a human body. She would have died if not for this blood, if not for ECMO, if not for the uncannily perfect timing of her transplanted lungs. There are some surgeons who might not have started ECMO if they had known how long Cindy would wait, weighing the possible complications against the chance of a good outcome.

But no one could have known that at the outset. So they did start ECMO, and Cindy got new lungs and she did not die.

Before I met Cindy, her doctors had described her to me as a poster child for ECMO. There is more to this description than one might think. First, it told me that Cindy had come close to death and that she was still alive thanks to high-level medical interventions. Not only had she survived; she was doing well. And she still is. She can walk and talk and think. Her outcome is undeniably a good one. She looks forward to her daughters' cheerleading competitions and sports games, she helps them with their homework, she and Derek can have entire conversations—days, even—that have nothing to do with sickness. Even the most mundane aspects of life, the fact that Derek has returned to work full-time and Cindy can brush her teeth at night and change into pajamas and wake up every day in her bed at home, are a daily testament to cutting-edge medicine and machinery. Cindy and her medical story are remarkable, the stuff of hospital fundraisers and made-for-TV movies. But being a perfect patient is work, and like celebrity, it is the kind of work that can wind up a burden.

Knowing this, I was initially hesitant to meet Cindy. Choosing to tell her story, of all stories, might be to ignore the darker aspects of this machine and the way that it can destroy a person, prolong an inevitable death, and devastate a family. I was concerned that Cindy might have been too lucky, that her story was too perfect and therefore not representative. But then in that first conversation, she showed me her scars. Survival wasn't as smooth as it might have looked when she walked in, coiffed and smiling, with her husband beside her.

And it occurred to me that even with her transplanted lungs, she was still holding her breath, waiting. Indeed, soon after Cindy and I first met, I learned that she was back in the hospital. It was her first hospital stay since her transplant, and she ended up on the same floor where she'd spent weeks after being transferred out of the ICU. She knew all the nurses and it was good to see them again, but it was disconcerting, too. This was the floor where she had come off the narcotics and anxiety meds she relied on while waiting for her lungs. She had been in pain there. When she left, she thought she had closed that chapter of her life for good. But there she was, once again hooked up to supplemental oxygen, the feel of the plastic prongs in her nose eerily familiar.

Derek spent the nights in the recliner next to his wife's bed, slipping into his habit of watching the peaks and valleys of her oxygen levels on the monitor. He did not sleep. It took them both back to the weeks and months of waiting for the transplant, to the fear and uncertainty that had characterized every moment. Cindy's children panicked, as if they believed their mother would never come home again. Though Cindy reassured them, she, too, felt on edge. She underwent a bronchoscopy, this time to look for a source of infection or evidence that her body was starting to reject her transplanted lungs. She tried to tell herself that she had taken good care of the new lungs, that she hadn't missed a medication and she had avoided infection, and things would be okay. But after all that had happened, she knew that none of it was really under her control.

It was only there in the hospital that Cindy ever mentioned the specter of rejection to me, and with it the reality that her transplant won't last forever—that no matter what she does, she might one day leave her children motherless. She had always known this, but something about that first admission since the transplant made it real. And even though Cindy was ultimately sent home feeling better and once again off oxygen—there was no rejection after all—she found that it was hard to bounce back. I wondered if she'd started to realize that this would be her new reality, stretches of relative normalcy punctuated by hospitalizations, each cough a reminder of the possibility of rejection.

"Maybe I'm just in a rut," Cindy told me one Saturday, a few weeks after her hospital stay, from the living room of the comfortable home where her family gathered for their usual weekend meet-up. The painful neuropathy that had plagued her since her transplant was at its worst that day after a few recent med changes. Her feet were numb and tingling, and searing pains shot through her legs when she touched them. She couldn't even sleep close to her husband at night. Cindy's youngest daughter, who had recently turned five, hung off her mother's arm, hesitant to leave the circle of adults even though her choice of cartoons played on the television upstairs. Cindy touched her daughter's hair gently as she tried to keep the child from lying on her legs. Her daughter had learned to be careful around what she called "Mommy's broken leg," although she'd occasionally forget.

Perhaps Cindy would feel better if she could get back to work. She had always enjoyed that part of her life, and found herself longing for the independence that came from making her own money. But she had been a geriatrics nurse who cared for patients in a nursing home, likely one of the worst jobs a new lung transplant recipient could possibly have. One of her older daughters had half jokingly suggested that she could become a school nurse. Cindy considered the idea briefly, but she worried that being exposed to sick kids wouldn't be any better. Maybe she could do paperwork in a doctor's office, if her transplant team gave her the okay. It would not be great but it would be something, at least. She would have to remember to call her doctors to ask.

There was a framed photo on the mantel under the television in Cindy's living room. In it, she stood in the ICU with her transplant surgeon, Dr. Camp. She was so weak back then that the surgeon had to use his arms to hold her body up. Cindy had returned to the unit where that photo was taken a few times, to see the doctors and nurses who had cared for her, but also to talk to patients on ECMO, waiting as she once was, to show them that things could get better. She brought them crossword puzzles and Sudokus, anything to keep their minds busy, and she tried to make them smile. It was hard for Cindy to be back there, but it felt important to do this, so she went.

I glanced from the woman in the photo to the woman across from me. She looked like a different person back then, and I told her so. I meant it as a compliment, and she smiled momentarily, but then she shook her head. She wasn't comfortable with the way she looked, she told me, not anymore. Even though she tried not to dwell on what she described to me as "these little things," it was jarring for her to see her body. She had recently met with a plastic surgeon to ask if he could do anything about the worst of the scars, the one on her abdomen from when she was bleeding there, but he said that after so many surgeries it would be risky to operate on that area.

There had been too much risk already. Cindy set the idea aside. She would wait, and maybe the scars would fade over time. Or perhaps she would grow accustomed to them until, little by little, they became a part of her.

7

Networking for a Kidney

Eddie Beatrice moved quickly, without hesitation. He gripped my hand and gave it a strong squeeze. As we sat, he pulled his smartphone out of his pocket and laid it on the table so he could keep track of the time. He had a doctor's appointment across the street and did not want to be late. I watched him for a second as he took a quick sip of his coffee. Eddie has a salesman's easy familiarity and a kind face, and as he set down his cup, I found myself wondering whether I would be willing to give this man a kidney.

I know. But it's not that strange a thought, in context. When Eddie was facing years on dialysis and the grim prospect of climbing a transplant waiting list, he had decided to take matters into his own hands and secure himself a kidney donor. A Google search, a few well-phrased e-mails, and a good deal of luck later, Eddie encountered a stranger across the country who said that she was willing to give him one of her organs. I found Eddie on the Internet as well, but we were meeting for a different purpose. I wanted to know what it took to do what he did—to consider the undesirable future his doctors had laid out for him, fistulas and fatigue and waiting, and to find another way forward.

In medical school, my classmates and I had the opportunity to sign up for two days with the transplant pager hooked to our belt. This meant that if someone in our geographic area died and that person was an organ donor, a shrill beep would sound. The lucky med student who was carrying the pager when it went off would travel with the surgeons to pick up the organ and return with it to New York City.

When it was my turn with the pager, I clipped it carefully onto the waist of my pants. I knew, somewhere within me, that I was waiting for someone to die, but I was excited nonetheless. And I was disappointed when the pager stayed silent for the entire forty-eight hours. Months went by before I finally saw a transplant.

Early one winter morning, outside the operating room, I pushed my curly hair into a cap, put on a mask and goggles, and scrubbed my hands with an uncharacteristic degree of fastidious attention. When I finished, I followed the surgeons into the OR and watched their choreographed movements as the scrub technicians dressed them in sterile gowns and gloves. The patient was already on the table, breathing tube in place, sedated by the milky white medicine that hung from the intravenous pole behind his head. I watched the surgeons carve a long incision into the patient's lower abdomen. I hadn't yet felt the sensation of using a knife to split flesh, and I found myself mimicking their motions with my own hand and wondering how much force they had to use. Then I watched as they divided the muscles that made up the abdominal wall and carefully dissected down to reveal blood vessels and bladder. I stood on a small metal lift, but even so, I had to crane my neck over the surgery fellow's head to see what was going on.

As I peered into the abyss of the abdominal cavity, the donor kidney appeared from somewhere behind me. I didn't know where it had come from, and when my view became obstructed again, my mind started to wander. I wondered about the man who lay there on the table in front of us and what sort of illness had brought him to this point. I wondered, too, about the kidney that was being sewn into his body and whether it had come from a friend or a family member or a stranger whose life had, perhaps just hours before, ended in tragedy.

"Make sure the med student gets to see this," I heard one of the surgeons say, and the gowned and gloved bodies in front of me parted so I could break from my daydream to observe the final step. "That's cool," I said, as the surgeons connected the donor's ureter, which is the tube that carries urine to the bladder, to the patient's bladder. These are a medical student's reflexive words of appreciation, but this time, thinking less about the surgical feat than about the fact that an organ had just been moved from one body to another right in front of my eyes, I meant it.

Soon after, on a similarly dark early morning, I observed

an organ harvest. A man lay on a stretcher in the operating room. He was brain-dead. The OR staff placed sterile drapes around his chest and abdomen. Then the surgical teams assembled. They were all from different hospitals, and they'd traveled here to take this man's organs back to patients waiting in their own institutions. I watched the surgeons as they opened the man's body with an incision running from his chest down to his abdomen, identified and clamped the vessels that had circulated his blood in life, and moved quickly to dissect out his organs and place them on ice. I saw his heart, his lungs, liver, and kidneys. I was transfixed.

It was cold in the operating room, and by the time the surgical team had sewn closed the body and left, the man was empty inside. I hesitated for a moment, alone with the gutted body and the organ donation coordinators, who by this time were debating whether to grab an early lunch at the Italian place down the street or go to one of the falafel trucks parked outside the hospital. When they settled on the Italian spot for subs and left, I stayed in the empty room alone. I was shivering.

Standing there, and then more fully later, I realized it wasn't the surgery itself that had grabbed hold of me. It was awesome, to be sure, and part of me will always love the routine and the theater of it all, the way the surgeons twirl around to close their gowns, the way the one in charge strode in wearing cowboy boots and selected his music—that day, classic rock. But what really held me captive there in the OR was something else. It was the weight of what had come before and what would come after. I wanted to understand what happened when an organ passed from one person to another, intertwining the lives of complete strangers. I wanted to learn about the odd relationships forged over kidneys, livers, and blood types, the messy place where illness, need, and inexplicable altruism coexist. Surgery was sterile, yet what intrigued me as I stood alone in that cold, empty operating room, and in the months and years to come, was anything but.

On the Friday of Columbus Day weekend in 2011, the year I finished medical school and started my internship, Eddie Beatrice checked into his local hospital. He was in his late forties at the time, happily married and living outside Boston with his wife and teenage son and daughter. Things were going well for him overall. He had recently decided to make a go of it and build his own sales and marketing e-commerce business. In his spare time, he'd picked up a boot-camp workout regimen and was getting "pretty svelte" for his age. When he went to see a doctor about the bothersome twinge that had become an ache in his shoulder, he learned that the decades of softball and hockey he'd played with his buddies had taken their toll and he'd need to undergo rotator cuff surgery. It would be inconvenient, as this sort of thing generally is, but the plan seemed simple enough—surgery in the fall, rest and recover through wintertime, ready for softball season by spring.

The surgery seemed to go smoothly, and he went home as scheduled. But he suffered through the weekend with an intense red-hot pain in his shoulder that was far more severe than he'd expected. He resolved to tough it out. By Monday, nauseated and retching until his stomach was empty, Eddie suspected he might be contending with more than simple postoperative pain. He continued to minimize his wife's concerns, hoping he would get better on his own, until the next morning, when he found himself too weak even to stand. His wife, an MRI technologist, had already left for work. As his daughter prepared to head off to school, she called upstairs. "Daddy, I'm going to school. Are you going to be okay?" *No,* he said to himself. He wasn't going to be okay at all. But he'd do anything to keep his daughter from worrying, so he told her to head to school, but to please give her mother a call on the way. By the time his wife walked through the door she found her husband pale, sweaty, and trembling. She helped him into the car and drove him straight to the emergency area of the local walk-in clinic. There, Eddie passed out.

Bacteria cascaded through his bloodstream. His vessels dilated and his blood pressure plummeted. Doctors ordered escalating doses of medications that worked directly on his heart to lift his blood pressure to the levels necessary to send blood to his brain and other organs. Thinking the nausea and vomiting of the previous day might be a clue as to what was going on, surgeons rushed Eddie into emergency surgery and opened his belly. They couldn't find any source of infection inside him, so they closed his body up again and transported the now unconscious man back upstairs to the ICU.

Days passed. He didn't improve. A priest came to administer last rites, and his children sat by his bedside, preparing to say goodbye to their father. Eddie's wife and her sister, grasping for something they could do to help, decided he needed to be transferred from the suburban hospital near their home into Boston, to "the best hospital in the world."

Even there, doctors were at a loss as to what kind of infection had initially ripped through Eddie's body, but slowly, his blood pressure stabilized. He could breathe without the tube. Eddie had lived. But as the haziness and delirium cleared, he learned that every other day someone would roll his stretcher out of his hospital room, into the elevator, and to another floor, where he would join a group of patients hooked to dialysis machines for hours at a stretch. He wasn't really sure what was going on or why, until his doctors told him that his kidneys weren't working. At first he assumed this, too, would pass. He resolved not to ask too many questions and to let the doctors do what they needed to do.

Eddie's doctors hoped that his kidneys had just been "stunned" by his devastating infection and shock, and that their function might return if they were given sufficient time to recover. The kidneys are sensitive organs, after all, and when the body gets sick and its blood pressure is low, they are often the first to show signs of damage. When Eddie started to make urine again, his doctors seemed excited. "That's a good sign, Eddie. That's a good sign," they told him.

Eddie relayed these optimistic updates to his wife and children. But the urine production was deceptive, and Eddie's kidneys were still too damaged to do their job of removing waste from his blood. By the end of December, Eddie's doctors had changed their message. They told him that his kidneys weren't going to recover after all. He didn't want to believe them, so for a time he underwent dialysis through a temporary catheter, unwilling to submit to the surgical procedure that would have connected an artery to a vein in his arm to create a fistula through which he could be dialyzed longer term. But despite Eddie's good nature, hopefulness, and dogged belief that things would be okay, his kidney function didn't come back. And slowly the reality set in—it wasn't going to.

When he finally returned home that winter, three months after his shoulder surgery, Eddie had lost forty pounds. Forget spring softball and the promise of the new company he'd been trying to build: he was too sick to do anything much during the day except wait for his next outpatient dialysis session. When his wife went back to work, his friends set up a rotation, driving Eddie to dialysis and then picking him up to return home. At the dialysis center he entered what felt like an alternate world, with long stretches of boredom punctuated by moments of fear. You would think being on dialysis is just about sitting still and waiting until it is over. That is certainly part of it. But from time to time Eddie's blood pressure would drop as his blood left his body to run through the dialysis machine, and he'd grow weak and his head would swim and he would end up in an ambulance on his way to the ER. Other times his body temperature would get out of whack and he would tremble so hard it seemed like a seizure. Most days, though, it was quiet. There was the television and the hope that he might be able to dull his mind and even fall asleep.

Eddie is friendly and open, and I imagine he was that way even when sick, so he got to know the other regulars in his dialysis time slot. Most of them were older than he and had been ill for a longer time. It struck Eddie that dialysis had become their job, and they seemed almost re-signed to that—it was simply what they needed to do if they wanted to stay alive. Sometimes, when a familiar face stopped showing up, Eddie would learn that the patient had died. A person could be there one session and gone the next, just like that. Eddie wondered whether this was how things would end for him, too. He imagined that he would die, and the people who shared his dialysis time slot might wonder where he was for a moment. Then someone else would fill his spot, and little by little the memory of his ex-istence would fade into nothingness.

But Eddie was only fifty. As soon as he grew strong enough that his body could handle the stress of another surgery, his doctors put him on the national waiting list for a kidney transplant. With that, his name joined those of more than eighty thousand men and women, some younger than Eddie and some older, some of their stories more tragic and some less, but all of them waiting for the same thing: a kidney from a person who had died. Wait times are different in different parts of the country, and in the Boston area, where Eddie was listed, his doctors told him he might wait five years or even more. He saw that future stretching out before him, dialysis for four hours at a stretch three times a week, weeks turning to months and then years. With all the potential complications, and an expected life span of only five to eight years after starting dialysis, Eddie couldn't even be sure he would live that long.

Positivity had always been important to Eddie, and from those early days in the hospital, he had resolved to act strong and soldier through. He wanted to show his children that he could face adversity and not give up. He wanted to inspire them. But the idea of waiting on that list, and the knowledge that he could die while waiting, rocked him. Only when he was alone, without his wife or children, did he let himself break down and cry.

Eddie's doctors had encouraged him to ask his friends and family if one of them would be willing to donate a kidney to him. It would be in his best interest to do so. First of all, kidneys from living donors generally function better than those from donors who've died. And if Eddie could find someone willing to give him a kidney, he wouldn't have to wait until he climbed to the top of the national waiting list. Besides, if anyone could make this happen, it would be Eddie. He'd been in sales his entire life, and his easygoing nature and charisma made him successful in that line of work. But Eddie didn't know the first thing about asking someone to undergo an elective surgery to remove an organ on his behalf, and the very idea left him with a sense of discomfort. So he didn't ask. Instead, he waited. He went to his dialysis sessions and he played solitaire or dozed off, and then he went home again. And the call did not come.

Weeks went by, then months. Maybe this was the way Eddie's life would be now. He could hope that his number would be called and pray that he would not get too sick while waiting. He could resign himself to this reality, like those he had seen around him in the dialysis center, and maybe he could even find a way to make pieces of it good. He found himself thinking that perhaps he could get back to work and help support his family, despite the constraints of his condition. But then, on New Year's Day of 2013, Eddie woke up and found that somehow his outlook had shifted. Things were different. He felt good that morning, better than he had in a while. He felt cocky. So he sat down in his living room in front of his computer, and he made a resolution. *"This is the year I'm going to get myself a kidney,"* he thought.

He didn't know how to do it. So he got started the way that any motivated, computer-savvy person would. He pulled up Google. He entered his search terms and started reading about kidney transplant and donation, following the links to a Facebook page for a nonprofit organization called the Living Kidney Donors Network. There he came upon a surprising message.

Just a few hours earlier, a woman living across the country in California had been sitting at home on her couch as the annual Rose Bowl parade played on television. Kelly Wright watched the Donate Life float pass across the screen. The float was packed with men and women, all there to honor family members who'd served as organ donors upon their deaths. Kelly saw people waving, and as the camera panned through the adoring crowds she found herself wondering why it was that she would have to wait until she died to give someone the gift of one of her body parts.

Kelly was forty-four years old with two small children. The idea of donating a kidney had actually come to her before, a few years back, when a friend's child developed kidney failure due to a congenital anomaly. She had been ready to give him one of her kidneys, but he ended up getting an organ through the national deceased donor waiting list. When Kelly was let off the hook, she was a little more disappointed than relieved, and the idea of donating stayed with her like an itch. That morning, something about seeing the float sparked her desire again, and this time, fueled by the promise of a new year and resolutions, she decided to make it happen. She, too, opened up her computer. She logged on to Facebook, found the Living Kidney Donors Network website, and sent a message off into the ether.

She wrote, *"A little scared but hopeful about saving a life!"*

That was it. Someone out there on the other end was going to get one of her kidneys. From across the country, in the living room of his home in a suburb outside Boston, Eddie read Kelly's message. He was just an hour and a half into his online search, and he hesitated. He read it again. "Is that what people do?" he asked himself. "I was new to this. I didn't know if I should respond. What's the protocol?"

Protocol aside, Eddie figured that if he didn't reply, someone else likely would. He hadn't realized that a complete stranger might offer to give up a kidney. It was surprising for sure, and it gave him pause, but the more he thought about it, the more appealing the idea became. Even if he ultimately found a friend or a relative who was able and willing to donate, he'd have to live with the knowledge that someone was going through an elective surgery, with all its risk, for him. But this woman was ready to give away a kidney. He couldn't imagine why, but it didn't really matter, did it? She had decided that she was going to donate to someone, and if it all worked out, he might as well be the one to get it. He began to craft a reply, anxious that in the minutes it took him to compose his message he'd lose his chance. Still uncertain of the protocol, he was careful to share enough to pique the writer's interest, but not so much that he might overwhelm her:

You are a very brave and giving person. I am a 51 year old male from North Reading, MA. I [have been] married to Julie for over 22 years and have two college age children...I also suffer end stage renal failure and require dialysis 3 days / 12 hours per week. My blood type is A+. I would love to be considered to be a recipient to receive your kidney. Please contact me if I might be considered and we can arrange a time to speak.

Respectfully, Eddie

After he sent the message he tried to quell his growing excitement. "I said, 'Well, what are the odds of that working out?'" So he kept the search going. He built himself a new Facebook page and a website that chronicled his shoulder surgery, the devastating infection, and his resultant kidney failure. He called the site and the Facebook page Eddie's Kidney Kampaign, choosing to spell "campaign" with a *K*. He wrote a brief bio and offered viewers a few pictures of himself with his family. He came across as a likable, regular guy.

And then a message popped up in his inbox. It was a response from the stranger in California.

"Hi Eddie...I think I am a universal donor...I certainly will help if I can!"

Far from the transplant clinics and doctor's offices, there

is a growing tide of men and women searching for organ donors through websites and message boards. This isn't the underground of buying and selling organs, although that, too, is real. There is nothing illegal about trying to look sympathetic on social media and hoping that you might be the winner of a stranger's generosity, although maybe there is something ethically murky about it. Some surgeons, uncomfortable with the way these relationships are formed, do refuse to operate on donor-recipient pairs who've found each other on social media. Still, I've seen posters in local coffee shops and in my hospital cafeteria. Take one recent example I came across while sugaring my coffee: a multigenerational family photo with the words *"Devoted father and grandfather needs a kidney, please call."*

Open Facebook any day and you can find them without leaving your bedroom; you can scroll through daughters and husbands and uncles and fiancées, lined up one after another like the strangest kind of dating site. They make their case with photos of loving families and dogs and babies, in tones alternately hopeful and pleading. I look through them and I wonder, *What if I were to pick one? Who would I pick? Why?* Some pages draw me in more than others. My eye goes to the ones with enough text, but not too much. I prefer photos and good grammar, as I do in a site that aims to find me a potential match of any sort, and in this case I also find myself searching for the stories that strike me as the most sympathetic. Maybe it would be the mother of an eight-year-old boy whose husband left her when she got sick. Maybe it would be the "regular twentysomething" who'd been thinking about law school until she wound up on dialysis. Or maybe it would be the man my father's age with a warm smile, "very well known around the community for being generous and giving back." Or would it be the gospel choir manager? Or how about the father of five who has dedicated his life to helping veterans? I could keep going. It doesn't end. There is so much need that it is almost hard to see it all. I struggle to imagine myself choosing among potential recipients and sending a message, and I find that I cannot.

Kelly is a different kind of person. She didn't hesitate. Eddie's story wasn't the most heartrending of all possible tales, but that wasn't what Kelly was looking for. Her motives were simpler than that; Eddie needed a kidney, and she wanted to give him one. In some way that defied words, giving her kidney to this particular stranger felt right, and Kelly just knew they were meant to meet. Kelly believes in fate, and she believed that this was the way things were supposed to work out.

She isn't one to change her mind once it's made up, not even after her father sat her down at Denny's and told her that she couldn't go through with the surgery. But Eddie didn't know this about her yet, and so he was more guarded. He decided to focus on building up his Eddie's Kidney Kampaign website. He picked a photo from his daughter's high school graduation for the cover shot. There he was, standing with his wife and daughter and son, looking proud in a white shirt and checked blazer. No one came forward through the website to offer to donate, but Eddie stayed with it. He had been through too much to put all his faith in a stranger who might not even be a match. Besides, even if she did end up with the medical okay to donate, he knew that up until the moment that she went under anesthesia and the surgeons made the first cut, she might get cold feet and back out. He wouldn't have blamed her.

Eddie had never met anyone quite like Kelly. He asked her why she wanted to give him her kidney. She told him, quite honestly, about how she had made her decision while sitting on the couch that day, watching the Rose Bowl parade. It was the truth, and she didn't intend to worry him, but that answer only concerned him more. Kelly had made up her mind so quickly, who was to say she wouldn't change it back just as fast? Eddie braced himself for disappointment, while a cousin of his started the work-up to become a donor.

But Kelly didn't disappear. To the contrary, she didn't seem to have any reservations at all. She texted Eddie frequently, messages that would come in nearly ten texts at a time, one after another in rapid succession, lighting up his phone throughout the day. Eddie, who tells me that he's "not really a phone guy or a text guy," always made sure that he was quick to respond. And as the weeks passed and he felt his comfort with the stranger who might donate her kidney grow, Eddie's feelings gave way to cautious optimism. When Kelly started planning to come to Boston at the end of February to get tested for her suitability as a donor, Eddie invited her to stay with his family. It was the least he could do. He planned a party for her, renting out half of a favorite restaurant about ten miles outside Boston. Dozens of people stopped by to meet the woman who might be able to return their friend to his former self, and when they all lined up to wish her well, Kelly felt like a celebrity. "I was overwhelmed. I never felt so loved in my life," she told me.

She still faced mixed reactions from friends who told her she was a fool to place her body in harm's way in order to give a kidney to a stranger. What if one of her children needed that kidney one day? What then? But she was moving forward and none of these hypotheticals would dissuade her. "You can't live with the 'what-ifs,'" she explained to me. "If we all lived like that, nobody would ever do anything. What if I die walking across the street? There are a lot of risks in life."

Kelly wanted to schedule the transplant as soon as possible. She was a match and she was healthy enough to donate, so she didn't see a reason to wait. Eddie was a little surprised and hesitant to allow her to move so fast, but as far as he could tell, Kelly was all for it. She seemed even more enthusiastic, or at least more vocal in her enthusiasm, than he was. They settled on a surgery date in April, just a month after she had secured the medical approval to become Eddie's donor.

With the date approaching, Kelly flew across the country

again, this time with her husband and mother. Eddie's house isn't huge, and there they all were under the same roof, the Wright clan squeezed into Eddie's daughter's bedroom. Those were a tense few days. The two families were still essentially strangers, but there they were, linked by need and altruism, one organ and two impending surgeries.

With all the medical tests and the phone calls and the texts and the travel that had led up to it, the day of the transplant was almost anticlimactic. It seemed that for Eddie and Kelly, the most complex and intricate negotiations had nothing to do, really, with what happened in the hospital. Kelly was wheeled in first, and then it was Eddie's turn. I asked Kelly to describe the surgery, and she paused mid-sentence. "The actual surgery? Oh, that was nothing," she replied. Kelly was up and walking around Boston to see the tourist attractions in just a few days.

For her, the hard part came later, when she returned home to California. There had been so much buildup, anticipation and planning and nervous excitement, and then, back home with the transplant over, it was so strangely quiet in comparison. Kelly was surprised that she didn't have more contact with Eddie. They'd been texting every day, multiple times a day, even, before the surgery. And of course she was busy as she worked to catch up on what she'd missed at home. But despite her other commitments, she found herself wishing that Eddie would take more initiative to maintain their relationship. "At the beginning, I felt a little touchy or upset when I didn't hear from him more often. There were some hurt feelings," Kelly told me.

It wasn't that Kelly needed people. She had, and still has, plenty: a time-consuming and fulfilling job as a cat veterinarian, a supportive husband, and two children. After the transplant, she had even started to care for an ailing homeless man in the little time she had free. And she had flown to Boston to donate her kidney without asking for anything in return. But only after it was all over and she was back home did she realize that maybe she had wanted something after all. Her kidney now lived inside Eddie. Did that very fact make them friends, or perhaps even family? Were they supposed to vacation together, or just call each other from time to time? Or maybe it meant nothing except that Kelly had done something extraordinary, and Eddie had been lucky, and that was all.

As for Eddie, he thought about Kelly often, with an amazed gratitude that he couldn't even put into words. What she had given him was the ability to live without dialysis and to return to his life, and that life was a busy one, with two children and a wife, and the hefty responsibility of a new job as a district sales manager for an industrial supply company. That needed to be okay with her.

Besides, it was not as if Eddie disappeared from Kelly's sphere entirely. He invited her back to Boston a few months after the surgery to join him for a walk to raise money for research on kidney disease. She stayed with his family again, and they all walked together, decked out in

T-shirts decorated with the words "Kelly's Heroes." They posed for photos with big smiles and their arms around one another. It was a great time. Kelly had given Eddie an organ. She hadn't done it to gain a friend or a family member, and as wounded as she initially felt, when it came down to it, she knew that. "It shouldn't come with anything I expected him to do," Kelly told herself. She didn't regret her decision. She would have donated again, if she could.

The twinge of disappointment in the nature of her relationship with Eddie might always be there. But it has faded over time as the donor and recipient have settled into a more comfortable pattern. Eddie refers to Kelly as his "little sister," though he is quick to note, with a smile, that he can go months without talking to his actual sisters. He and Kelly do talk from time to time, to check up on how things are going or to acknowledge birthdays and holidays. After all, they will always be linked. Eddie describes his kidney as a "she," and thinks frequently of the possibility of rejection, dutifully swallowing a dozen pills each day to make sure that his body accepts Kelly's organ for as long as possible.

It's been years since his transplant, but Eddie intermittently receives requests from people on the transplant waiting list for advice on how they, too, might secure an organ donor. He tries to reply to each of them. It feels like a kind of responsibility. After all, he figures that they aren't going to get any of this information in the doctor's office. So he shares with them what he learned of the human mess of hope and fear that lines the path to the operating room. Behind the scenes, it is all so much more complicated than I ever could have anticipated. "When you're starting a kidney campaign, you need to attack it like you're searching for a job. You need to send out your 'résumé,'" he tells them. That means you need to develop the right kind of online presence: tone is important, and don't write too much. You need to keep a positive attitude, and you should never complain on your website. That's key. For example, it would be reasonable to describe a day on dialysis as "another four hours on dialysis. Ugh." But if Eddie were to write that, he would make sure to follow it with a more uplifting message in order to keep his readers engaged. For instance, he could end with something like "Still better than the alternative."

The most important tip when it comes to getting an organ donor? That's a lesson Eddie initially picked up while working in sales, and it has little to do with any of what I learned about organ donation back in medical school, years ago. "It's about networking," he told me earnestly, before he got up from our coffee to head to his doctor's appointment. "You need to network, network, and network some more."

8

An Unexpected Adulthood

The teenager tapped her foot as she waited in the examining room. Meghan Kiley had been going to see her doctor every three months for as long as she could remember. When she was younger, the visits were actually enjoyable. Sure, he listened to the sounds of her lungs, pressed on her belly, and used a bright light to peer into her eyes and ears. But he also made her laugh, and he quizzed her on the history facts she'd learned in school and asked her questions about what she wanted to be when she grew up. The pediatrician told Meghan that she would be the boss of something someday, and he spoke about her future with such certainty that she believed him.

Because it was her reality, and because her parents tried to shield her from their worry, she assumed that everyone her age went to the doctor as frequently as she did. She had to take pills with her meals, but so did her friend who was lactose intolerant. She didn't feel fragile. She had no idea that her father stayed up during the night listening to her coughing jags, half worried that she would stop breathing. She played volleyball, took ballet lessons, went off to camp in the summer.

By the time she turned fifteen, Meghan had long ago learned about cystic fibrosis, this invisible thing inside her that would mandate her daily attention for the rest of her life. She knew that her mother, who accompanied her to every single appointment, kept a binder full of her pre-scriptions and insurance paperwork—a responsibility that Meghan would one day have to take on for herself. She knew that in order to stay healthy, she would have to keep track of her meds and stay on top of her physical therapy, day after day and year after year. But in a moment of what she could only explain as an ill-conceived act of adolescent rebellion, Meghan had skipped the pills she was supposed to take with meals to replace her pancreatic enzymes.

The pain in her stomach was excruciating; Meghan would not miss a pill again. But she still had to do penance. Her regular doctor was away, so she would see one of his colleagues to review what had happened.

The door opened. Her pediatrician generally entered the room with a warm, easy smile and a ready joke no mat-ter how busy his schedule. In contrast, this doctor's air was serious, his manner businesslike and almost cold. He examined her—stethoscope on her chest, hands on her abdomen. She was used to that routine. Then, as the visit wound to a close, something unexpected happened. The doctor took out a piece of paper and a pen, and proceeded to draw a simple graph. Meghan watched, uncertain where this would lead. He labeled one axis of the graph as time and the other how he anticipated her lung function would decline. He showed her where she was on the graph that day at age fifteen. He then traced the line out fifteen more years, to Meghan's thirtieth birthday. This, he said, was when her lungs would fail and she would likely "expire." The doctor drew a dot there at thirty to mark her expiration date, and then he circled the dot. Her surprise quickly turned to fury. Meghan knew she had CF, but no one had ever talked to her about death before. Time, which had seemed infinite, shrank and collapsed into that dot. Meghan's face reddened, her anger louder than her fear.

That day, she promised that when she turned thirty, she would enjoy the sweetest victory her fifteen-year-old self could imagine—a huge party. She would invite all her doctors and nurses and friends, and she would show them that she had made it; she was still alive.

Meghan Kiley was born one year before me, in 1980. Perhaps because we are around the same age, I find that as I re-create the story she told me about that years-ago appointment and fill in the details, I'm tempted to place my own fifteen-year-old self in her position. Yet as much as I try, it is so far from my reality that it's almost foolish to imagine how I would have reacted. After all, I spent much of my adolescence studying, planning, and preparing for a future so distant that I couldn't even make out its shape. That dot at age thirty was just about where I thought my life would truly begin—with money, security, maybe a family. Had someone told me that my genetics meant an early death, I think I still would have gone to college if I had been healthy enough. Though it's impossible to know, really, I doubt I would have decided to spend years in a lecture hall postponing adulthood in the hope of becoming a doctor. But maybe I would have. Maybe I would have felt the exhilarating pace of medical progress and realized that when I was born, babies with cystic fibrosis weren't expected to live through adolescence, but there I was—alive. Perhaps I would have been optimistic or foolish enough to bet on a future that I might or might not get to enjoy.

Meghan knew she was going to college. There was no question. Though her father wanted her to go to school down the road so she could live at home, she craved the real campus experience. It felt important for her to get away, and it felt important for her not to mention her diagnosis anywhere in her application. But cystic fibrosis was there, too, traveling the forty minutes from her home to her Providence College dorm and lingering in the background of the college life she worked to build. A physical therapist showed up at her room five times a week without fail to clap on Meghan's back while she held different positions, loosening the mucus that accumulated in her lungs. When friends asked whether the woman visiting Meghan so often was her mother, she nodded. A nervous mother's frequent visits were easier to explain than illness.

Time was a strange thing. Meghan wasn't really sure how

to think about approaching her twenties. If she were truly to believe the graph that doctor had created and the future it foretold, she was entering her final decade and time was short. But other than the infrequent hospital admission for pneumonia, and the intravenous lines and antibiotics that inevitably came with it, Meghan's daily reality was one of a young woman at the start of her adulthood. Maybe it was because her parents had never treated her as though she would break, maybe it was because her pediatrician had always encouraged her to look toward the future, or maybe it was just because of her own stubborn personality, but Meghan moved forward. She didn't see any other choice. She finished college, made plans for graduate school, and decided to move to New York, where she knew no one. She found roommates on Craigslist to share a place on Long Island, and with her family (and her doctors) no longer a short drive away, it felt as if she had traveled to a different world.

And yet at the same time, Meghan found herself making subtle compromises. She strikes me as a planner—the type who would begin saving for a down payment on a house even in her twenties. But she didn't save. Instead, she used her money to go on vacation. After all, she thought, what was the point of putting all this money aside for the future if she wouldn't get to use it? She dated, but never anyone who was good to her and serious about a relationship. She had always loved being around children. But given her conviction that she wouldn't live long enough to have her own family, she figured she would find ways to satiate her maternal impulse by working in college education and helping other people's children. Still, the years passed, one into another. And fifteen years after she sat in that clinic watching a doctor draw a graph, she was planning a thirtieth birthday party.

It was as she'd imagined, outdoors on a sparkling summer day under a huge tent at her family home on Cape Cod. Meghan's mother had died of breast cancer a few years before, but her father was there, and her family and friends and even some of the doctors and nurses who'd taken care of her. There was a DJ, a dance floor, catered food, a hot-pink-and-lime-green color theme. After dinner, a party bus came to transport the group to a nearby bar, where they continued to dance into the early hours. To Meghan, who assumed she would never have the chance to get married, this party felt like her equivalent of a wedding. It was perfect. But when she woke up the next day and the day after that still feeling healthy, she slowly felt herself facing a strange and surprising question: "Now what?"

How long would this reprieve last? She surely could have become paralyzed by that uncertainty. One woman with cystic fibrosis, approaching her fortieth birthday, explained that she had framed her life around the belief that she would die in her teens. After all, that was the expectation for those with the disease when she'd been born. Growing up to focus on the "now," she never considered what an adulthood might actually look like. She never pursued a job. She surely never imagined aging, or outliving her grandparents. With new drugs and advances in infection control, though, she was doing just this, and remarkably well. But she was lost.

A man in his early thirties started a new drug that targets one of the genetic defects responsible for the symptoms of cystic fibrosis. He was lucky. He had the right mutation, and the drug was working for him. He married, even had children. But every day he took that pill he feared it was the day it would stop working. It was as though he were waiting for the moment when his doctor's prophecies from decades ago came true and he would die.

Another young woman described a turning point when she decided she should start wearing sunscreen. She was still unsure about how much she could plan for her future. But it looked like she just might be around long enough for accumulated sun damage to matter. When your life expectancy continues to shift within your lifetime, it's hard to know what to envision. You can't help but shuttle between anxiety and fear on the one hand, and cautious optimism and hope on the other.

It was a Monday evening. I had traveled to North Attleboro, a town south of Boston, to meet Meghan and her husband, Myles, in the home they shared with their Chihuahua. When Meghan answered the door I took in her fair skin and delicate features, brown hair in a neat shoulder-length cut. I never would have guessed her diagnosis. I'd arrived a few minutes before her physical therapist, so we would have time for a brief tour of the house that she and Myles had recently bought. The living room struck me as something out of a magazine, cozy but not cluttered, color coordinated and decorated with a chalkboard on the wall bearing the legend "There are only two options: Make progress or make excuses" in big block letters. The bedroom, bathroom, living area, and kitchen are all on one level, she noted, which was a selling point when they were looking to buy. One day, when walking has become hard, Meghan will still be able to make her way through her house without having to struggle up stairs.

She doesn't know when that day will come, but she works tirelessly to stave it off as long as possible. As a child, she only had to take a few pills each day. But with each passing decade the medical burden had grown, and it sometimes seemed as though her entire life had become structured around keeping sickness at bay. It was exhausting just to think about. This month, the regimen involved thirty minutes of an inhaled antibiotic in the morning and at night. (Never one to waste time, Meghan took up knitting to pass the sixty minutes of imposed stillness and recently made a hat.) During alternating months her doctors switch her to a different inhaled antibiotic three times a day—easier in some ways because each of the treatments is shorter, but harder because her midday dose leaves her scrambling to find a place at work to give herself the treatment without anyone watching through her office window.

There were other meds over the years. Her doctors stopped a nebulizer with a high-salt solution when she started coughing up blood, and she traded the vibrating vest for exercise as a more effective method to help clear her lungs. Then there are pills, of course, pills in the morning and with snacks and meals. Also paperwork, insurance claims, reimbursements. She spends a few hours each week on the phone with the mail-order pharmacies that supply her meds, and it seems as though she's constantly dealing with calls for prior authorization, trying to temper her frustration as she navigates the maze of the medical system. She remembers the binders full of diligent notes her mother kept during her childhood, and as hard as it is, she stays organized. Even so, it's like having another job, she told me. "In the weirdest way, it's a normal life because it's normal for me," she explained as I struggled to write it all down. "But no one else in my life other than my husband has any idea just how much work it is."

Meghan brought out a few large throw pillows from a closet and lay on her couch while Jen, the physical therapist who had arrived while we were talking, took her spot on the floor. At first it looked a little like a massage. Jen cupped her hands and slowly, rhythmically, clapped Meghan's back. While she worked, the two women chatted and laughed with the easy familiarity of friends catching up over drinks. Myles headed down to the basement to watch some television in quiet, the dog following eagerly after him. The scene was homey and comfortable, and I felt myself start to relax into the couch. But when Jen finished liberating mucus from one lobe of Meghan's lungs and she sat up, gave a deep cough, and spat sputum into a cup, the world shifted and it was a medical procedure once again.

This intrusion of the highly medical into everyday life is unavoidable, and it is something that Meghan knows will increase over time. She tried to keep that part of her life from Myles when they first started dating, on one occasion even concealing an intravenous catheter under her shirt and leaving his house at 2 a.m. to dose her IV antibiotics while driving back to her home. She had finally worked up the nerve to tell him about her cystic fibrosis over drinks at a bar, and when she broke the news he shrugged, or at least that's how Meghan remembers it. Myles didn't know much about cystic fibrosis back then, he told me, and so he wasn't quite sure how to react. But he would learn.

When Myles started talking about the future, some months after those first dates, Meghan told him to "pump the brakes." Before she could begin thinking of any kind of commitment, she wanted him to see everything. She needed him to know that CF was more than a box of pills and nebulizers and physical therapy, which meant that he would need to see her in the hospital. The winter after they first met, Meghan got sick and was admitted, as she is most winters, for IV meds and inhaled treatments. She is usually assigned to one of the highest floors of the hospital, where the walls are wood paneled, the rooms large, and the nurses familiar. I visited during an admission like that. Meghan was receiving intravenous antibiotics, and I had to wear a yellow contact isolation gown and gloves to enter. But she was dressed in an oversized Ruth Bader Ginsburg–themed "Notorious RBG" T-shirt and leggings, bickering comfortably with her father about why he had thought she would want a tray of cupcakes in the room. (For her visitors, he replied.)

During the admission the winter after she met Myles, though, for some reason she ended up being sent to a room on a lower floor. The nurse referred to her as a "CFer," a term that has always rubbed her the wrong way. Perhaps slightly anxious about the stakes involved in introducing Myles to the realities of cystic fibrosis, Meghan decided she would defuse the stress of the situation and have some—admittedly goofy—fun. When he sat at the side of her bed, she shrieked in mock horror, pretending he'd pulled out her IV. On another occasion, she hid in the bathroom and surprised him. He recovered nicely after a moment's panic. And he stayed.

Myles had fallen hard for Meghan's smile, infectious enthusiasm, and intense energy. By the time he proposed, cystic fibrosis had become a part of his life. He understood the serious nature of his wife's diagnosis, he told me. In the back of his mind, he was conscious of the possibility that she could get sick at any time. Myles, a middle school phys ed teacher, has an air of unflappable, perpetual calm (in fact, one of Meghan's doctors described him as "her rock"), but he admitted to me that he probably seems far more laid-back about the disease than he actually is.

Meghan's most recent hospital stay had scared him. It had scared her, too. She had gotten sick—really sick, a fever to 105, unable to get out of bed—due to an abscess, a walled-off infection, in her lung. Doctors gave her one antibiotic after another, each name and potential side effect profile longer than the last. Usually, a few days into an admission, Meghan feels good enough to have friends come by, order in pizza, and act as if the hospital room is a spa. But this time was different. Her kidney function worsened. She needed supplemental oxygen. She could barely walk. She only allowed members of her immediate family to visit.

When Meghan finally made it home, she was far weaker and thinner than when she'd left, and she was shaken by how sick she'd become. Though she had been out of the hospital for a few months by the time we met, she still hadn't rid herself of the feeling that she was "living on a razor's edge." It seemed that something had shifted. There was no dot on a chart to tell her when, but she knew her lung function would decline. Her admissions would escalate in frequency and severity. This would all happen again and it could be worse, no matter how much she washed her hands and exercised, even if she never skipped a treatment. That was the future. One day she might have to think seriously about the possibility of a lung transplant.

So Meghan had started to wonder what it would be like to cut down on work or even to retire completely. Work had been part of her identity since graduating from college, and I imagine that her job—as the associate director of student success and retention at Providence, where she'd gone to college—was a key aspect of not feeling defined by sickness. But the days on campus were long and tiring, packed with meetings and undergraduates who needed her attention. While these were all things Meghan loved, she wasn't sure how long she would have enough energy to devote herself fully to work while staying on top of the increasingly arduous task of managing her disease.

She found herself wondering how she would reply when someone asked her, "What do you do?" It had once seemed like such a simple question. She offered some potential answers that night as Jen worked her way down her back. Would she say, "Nothing"? Would she say she had retired? She paused for a moment. She would need more time to find the language that sounded right.

As we sat in her living room, the clap of Jen's hands on Meghan's chest in the background, I couldn't help but once again project my own self and ambitions onto her. That's a foolish thing to do, of course. I can't really understand her experience, as I grew up with the sense that life and time are essentially limitless, while Meghan had long been aware that the good part might be shorter than she hoped. Even so, she had been healthy long enough to go full force at a career, and she had found a field in which she excelled and work that felt perfect for her. In her midthirties she'd reached a point at which she should have been able to enjoy accolades and advancement. In a way, it all should have just been starting. Instead, when her boss asked her to sit on a national committee or teach courses, she said no, even though she wanted to jump at the opportunities. Reality intruded. She wasn't sure what her lung function would be like in the year to come, or when she would next be admitted to the hospital and for how long. Cystic fibrosis had always been in her life, to be sure, mandating that she wash her hands regularly, that she not come into close contact with others who had the disease lest their germs pass on to her. But it had never so clearly limited her life's course until now.

Before the shock of her most recent hospitalization, she and Myles had been thinking, cautiously, about trying to have a child. She'd always assumed pregnancy to be off-limits. It is hard to plan to build a family if you expect to die not too long after your thirtieth birthday. But at a visit with a high-risk obstetrician, Meghan and Myles learned that she actually had no strict medical contraindication to carrying a baby, and slowly, it seemed, the couple had allowed optimism to creep in. They had started to imagine the possibility. Maybe they could have a family. Then she got sick, and though she made it home and was back at work and gaining weight, with her friends asking when she was going to start "popping out babies," she felt uncertain.

What would pregnancy do to her tenuous lung function? What if she got sicker the next time and was unable to rebound?

When Meghan thought aloud about adoption, Myles, ever supportive, encouraged her to explore the possibilities, but she wasn't sure adoption was the answer, either. Even without the physical stress of pregnancy, her lung function would worsen, possibly taking with it her ability to mother the way she would want. She and Myles had talked about this. He knew he might have to take on more and more parental responsibility if her health declined, and he knew, too, that he might be left to parent alone. After seeing him with his students, she trusted that he would be a great father, and it was an experience she wanted for him. Even so, the reality of it all was hard to fathom. When Meghan's mother died, it had gutted her. How could she decide to bring children into a family, knowing that she might grow sick and leave them?

Meghan had outlived the expiration date her doctor had given her. She had marked so many milestones that were far from certain when she was a child—she went away to college, lived alone, dated while on intravenous antibiotics, married. She had even started to think about her previously unimaginable fortieth birthday (no party this time, just a dinner at a nice restaurant). But maybe having a child was something she wouldn't be able to do. Maybe going to work each day, coming home and eating dinner with her husband, maybe that was enough for now. She was grateful for these "average" things that she loved, she told me. Maybe there didn't need to be anything more.

She was quiet for a moment. I listened to the rhythmic sound of Jen's hands against Meghan's chest. I listened to her cough and heard the spit land in the cup. She would do it all again the next day and the day after that. "Right now, I feel good," Meghan offered, smiling. She had managed a treadmill run earlier that day. And there were things to look forward to. In seven weeks, she and Myles were heading to Mexico for a vacation. Though she worried about leaving her comfort zone for the trip, uncertain what would happen if she got sick or needed her doctors, she planned to fill her Kindle with books and enjoy the time away. It would be sunny and the sand would be warm. "I like to travel, and I don't know how much time anyone has," she told me. "So what choice is there?"

A few days after I visited Meghan, I worked an overnight shift in the ICU. The intern and I were sitting at our computers, scanning lab results, when one of the cystic fibrosis specialists walked into the unit. Surprised, I glanced at the time on the computer screen. It was just after 11 p.m.—she should have been home hours ago. It was clear she'd had a rough day. Her mascara was a little smudged, her skirt crumpled, and she walked with her shoulders slumped. She sat down next to us and exhaled loudly. "I have an admission for you," she said. I gestured to the intern to start taking notes.

The patient was a thirty-seven-year-old man with CF, she told us. That meant he was just about Meghan's age—and just about my age, too. But he was dying. Perhaps due to his own genetics, perhaps due to bad luck and bacteria, his disease had taken a severe course. He had been in the hospital for over a month, battling infection after infection. Now his lungs, destroyed by nearly four decades of the disease, could barely work to exchange oxygen for carbon dioxide without a machine strapped to his face to blow air in and push it out. Even with the machine he was on the edge, and he might need to be intubated. I nodded slowly, taking in the story. "Probably there's nothing we can fix," the specialist told us. The patient wasn't ever going to get a lung transplant—he was too weak to tolerate the surgery, and his other organs were failing, too—so there was no backup plan.

Sitting in the quiet of the ICU workroom, I felt fairly sure that this patient was nearing the end of his life. But outside the room things were more complicated, and there was a young man who did not want to die. He would come to the ICU, and we would give him more and stronger antibiotics and hope there was some way we could make him better. "This sounds like a terrible situation," I said. My words felt insufficient. "Thanks for that heads-up." I imagined him dying under my watch that night. I took a deep breath. "You should go home!" I told her. "We'll take care of him."

About twenty minutes later, our patient's stretcher rolled

through the doors, pushed by his nurses from the general medical floor. I took him in as he moved past. He was small and too thin, curled up on his side on the stretcher. I thought of how it must have been for him as a child, how no one expected him to live to be thirty or thirty-five, and how he had celebrated these birthdays that weren't supposed to come, one after the other. As the years passed, I imagined, hope may have started to appear around the edges.

I followed the stretcher to his room and stood at the side of his bed. His limbs were skinny and muscles wasted, skin so pale it was almost gray, eyes rimmed with bluish circles. He was too weak to walk. The machine he wore to help him breathe had been on his face so long that it had left red indentations in the thin skin on the bridge of his nose. He had made it to thirty-seven with cystic fibrosis, lived nearly a decade he wasn't due to live, in a daily testament to the sparkling forward march of medical advance. But at the moment when I met him that night and pressed my stethoscope to his skeletal chest to hear his heart racing, none of that seemed to matter. I stood at the side of the bed and there was only a man who could not breathe without a machine strapped to his face. There was only the rapid beating of his heart, the smell of sweat and sickness, and the sadness that shook me, all of a sudden, because thirty-seven is still young, and he was dying.

When I first decided to write about cystic fibrosis, I thought

I would focus on the genetic therapies that promise to drastically change this disease, or perhaps on the new rules of infection control that prohibit one person with CF from being in the same room as another. I reached out to a handful of experts, and about a week after I met Meghan and admitted the man with cystic fibrosis to the ICU, I sat down with Dr. Ahmet Uluer, who directs the Adult CF Program at Boston Children's and Brigham and Women's Hospitals. By then I had started to think about the disease in a context far broader than cutting-edge treatments and improved infection control. Still, I wanted to understand the changes that were on the horizon.

Dr. Uluer and I met for coffee and then headed over to talk among the books and Legos in his small but comfortable Children's Hospital office. On that day, Uluer was dressed slightly more formally than the everyday doctor's garb of chinos, button-down shirt, and fleece jacket, and as we walked, he mentioned that he was going to a patient's funeral that afternoon. He tries to make it to each of his patients' funerals, he told me. His wife had gone to the first one, but she cried so much (more than the patient's mother, he remembered) that she hadn't been able to go with him again. He also writes an obituary with colorful details about the person's life and sends it out to the cystic fibrosis team via e-mail. That way, his colleagues all know when a patient has died and will remember a little something about the person.

The funeral he was going to that day was for my thirty-seven-year-old patient. I had last seen him the morning after my shift, when he was no better but no worse, either, and I didn't know that he had died. When Dr. Uluer told me, I wasn't sure how to react at first. I had come to talk with him about advances in CF therapies, but there I was, remembering that room and thinking about endings. I asked how it had happened, and I learned that the young man's breathing grew more labored, and ultimately, in the last choice he was able to make, he opted to die without a breathing tube.

I wanted to know more about him. Dr. Uluer told me that he'd had a great, often crude, sense of humor. I didn't learn this during our brief interaction in the middle of the night, when he hadn't shown me his personality and I hadn't asked him to. But he'd been hospitalized so many times that everyone on the cystic fibrosis team knew him and genuinely enjoyed coming to see him on rounds. Even when his body was failing and he was sick and angry that he was dying, he was still himself, cracking jokes in his hospital room. *The Godfather* was his favorite movie, and he held court in the ICU like Don Corleone himself, motioning each visitor to sit by his side. He set up an espresso machine he'd brought into each of his hospital rooms over the years, and on what would become the last morning of his life, he had savored a sip.

I could tell that Dr. Uluer would miss this patient. He misses them all. And even though our conversation did ultimately turn to advances in CF treatment and to the small-molecule therapies that might one day transform this disease, the tone had changed. Yes, there are more adults than children living with this disease, and one day there will be geriatric cystic fibrosis clinics, and the letters CF will stand for "cure found." The energy is palpable, and it is exciting. But the reality of that day was about something different. On that day, Dr. Uluer was going to a funeral for a thirty-seven-year-old man. And as we talked, it occurred to me that all of this—the man who had died, Meghan and Myles, their hopes and expectations and disappointments—this is cystic fibrosis today. It's discovery and game-changing new drugs, some of which have come and others that are just beyond our reach. It's babies born with life expectancies that likely will extend during their own lifetimes, who will grow up healthier than anyone could have imagined decades ago. It's throwing a party on the thirtieth birthday you were told you wouldn't have and building a career and falling in love and buying a house before you turn thirty-five, but making sure that house has only one floor because there could—no, there will—be a day in the not-too-distant future when you are too sick to walk up the stairs. It is learning that you are healthy enough to carry a child but being scared to go through with it because you do not know if you are healthy enough to watch that child grow. It is a young man just about my age dying in the ICU, and a doctor preparing to go to his funeral. It is possibility and time, opening and extending longer than expected, but not long enough.

9

How It Begins

In the world of the hospital, July 1 is all movement and nervous energy.

It's a beginning and an ending, as this is the day that medical students become doctors, interns become residents, and fellows start the first real jobs of their lives. On July 1 almost fourteen years ago, I walked hesitantly into an anatomy lab to meet a cadaver named Murray whose body I would disassemble and commit to memory. Fourteen years is long enough to have a child and to watch that child finish middle school. It's long enough to get a job and buy a house and grow disenchanted and leave your job for something new. In that time, you can marry and divorce, start dating and marry again. But I did none of these things. I lived in two cities and six apartments. I finished medical school and officially became a doctor. I went on to train as a resident in internal medicine and then as a fellow in critical care. I stopped writing in order to devote myself wholly to memorization, and then, when I missed it too much, I started to write once again. I learned which supply closets on which hospital floors have the best crackers—Ritz, not saltines—and the freshest little tubs of peanut butter. I learned to go to work each day surrounded by sickness and death and to recognize the sadness, but not to let it paralyze me. I learned to diagnose and treat, to connect and communicate. And then it was over; one day I was a doctor in the midst of my infinite training, and the next I was an attending physician, that faraway goal finally a reality.

The shift was almost imperceptible. I wasn't changing hospitals. I had already started working as the physician-in-charge overnight in my hospital's intensive care unit. I had to change my health insurance benefits, but I needed no new passwords or computer access to do so. I didn't even get a new hospital identification card. And yet something real had happened. It had been a luxury to spend all these years just a step away from command, always a little bit the observer, enjoying the buzz of responsibility without its weight. Part of me wished that stage of my life could have lingered on indefinitely. But time moves, and I moved with it.

Which is how, one afternoon in early July, I came to sit in the examining room of the transplant outpatient clinic. As a junior faculty member I've been assigned duties that take me out of the intensive care unit and to the margins, to the realms of after and before. I spend some weeks each year caring for ventilated patients at our affiliated long-term acute care hospital, and in my outpatient clinic I see people whose doctors have referred them for consideration of lung transplant. These outpatient visits are unique. We have the luxury of time. We can sit. I review the records. We talk. And based on a handful of absolute rules and a few more subjective ones, we determine whether a patient can proceed on the path toward becoming a candidate for transplant. I think of this visit as a key inflection point. Illness is real and present, yet I meet these men and women early, before they have to make the decisions that set them on a path toward uncertain outcomes.

Often I have learned about decisions through hindsight, from what comes after. But this clinic is different. The after hasn't yet come to pass. Whether a transplant ever becomes reality, this clinic marks the beginning—before the consent forms, the surgery, the prolonged recovery, before the possibility of tracheostomy tubes and long-term acute care hospitals, before the return home with prescriptions and pills and appointments and anxiety. This is how it all starts, in a clinic waiting room on an ordinary afternoon.

It was a Wednesday. Six people sat in a semicircle in a small meeting room in the outpatient clinic space, watching an informational video about the transplant process. I pulled up a chair to the outside of their circle and sat, looking in. I would introduce myself as the doctor later, but at the moment I wanted just to be present. There were three pairs, each made up of a patient and a family member: two husbands and wives, one mother and daughter. The woman next to me sat in a wheelchair. Her oxygen tank hissed softly. Halfway through the video, the battery of her tank must have given off some warning, because she rummaged in her bag and pulled out the kind of cord you'd use on a computer. Her husband stood up and helped her unravel the cord, looking around for a wall socket. "There's a plug over there," one of the patients offered. "There's one over here, too," someone else said. All three patients might one day be on the same transplant list hoping to be the recipient of a scarce resource, but nonetheless, at least in those early moments, there was camaraderie in the room, a sense of shared destiny that linked these strangers as they peered into the future. The cord reached an outlet, and with the oxygen tank safely plugged into the wall, the group relaxed and turned back to the video.

In each pair, the healthy one sat at attention, eyebrows furrowed with worry, pen in hand, scribbling in a notebook or on scrap paper. In transplant, the need for a loved one is actually codified—at my hospital's lung transplant program, a support system of at least three people is required before you'll be considered for an organ. I flashed to the future for a moment and saw how these roles could become calcified in the months and years that would follow. The husband or wife or daughter would be the one who clarified details for the doctors and recorded lab values and asked questions and kept folders and remembered appointments and picked up prescriptions and spent nights in the family room wrapped in that scratchy, too-thin hospital blanket, waiting. There would be so much waiting.

The video did not sugarcoat. There were no transplant recipients extolling the virtues of transplantation. The time for that would come later. Here, patients learn that they will take more than a dozen different medications daily. They'll need a full-time caregiver for at least the first few weeks after transplant because they can't be alone, not even while asleep, and they'll need others who are willing to commit their time to pick up food or drive to appointments. They learn that in most cases, the primary goal of lung transplant isn't to make life longer, but instead to improve its quality. Nearly half of all lung transplant recipients die within five years. Moving forward would mean exchanging a known set of problems for an unknown set that we all hoped would be better but understood might not be.

When I first learned about this clinic, I had thought my job would be to make sure that my patients knew precisely what they were getting into before they moved ahead. To some extent, that's the right idea. We give survival statistics in the video, explain how many medicines our patients might have to take, and warn them and their families that for the first months or even a year or longer, recovery can be harder than they would have ever imagined. We tell them that even if they are facing complication after complication and their bodies do not feel like their own any longer and they have not been home for months, their doctors will encourage them to move forward until they have reached the true limits of possibility. They have a responsibility not just

215

to themselves, but also to the transplanted lungs that now live inside them.

If they have specific questions about the nature of the surgery or the side effects of the meds, we answer those or we refer them to someone who can. Most important, I think, beginning with that video, we explain that transplant is not a panacea. None of the things we do are, not an ICU stay or an implantable device or a state-of-the-art medication. If our patients think that modern medicine can make things perfect, they're doomed to disappointment. What we offer is never a true cure but a different sickness, albeit a preferable one, we hope, to the one they are battling. So we lay out these broad expectations. We realize that they might not even really hear them today, on the first visit. There will be countless conversations over the coming weeks, months, even years. But if we do it well, maybe there's something familiar when they hear it again. Maybe that's the best we can do.

The video ended. The group was quiet. One of the clinic staff led each person down a hall and into an examining room, and I left to scan their charts. I gathered some details about my first patient: she had a dog; her adult children lived across the country; she smoked marijuana when she was in college but just a few times, because it didn't agree with her; she ate a scoop of ice cream for dessert but not every night; and she had been on oxygen for four years. I tried to hold those little details she had chosen to share with us in my head so that I would make her feel as though this doctor she had never seen was someone she could trust.

I glanced at my watch. I had been reading slowly, and I was seven minutes late. I thought of her sitting in the examining room for those seven minutes, uncomfortable and nervous, perhaps wondering if she should just leave, and I told myself to hurry. I gathered my papers, doused my hands with Purell, and swung open the door. My patient was looking at her phone. She began to stand when I walked in, but I could see the oxygen tubing already half tangled around the legs of the chair, and I told her not to worry. I shook her hand. Mine was cold, and hers was hot and a little bit sweaty from waiting in the stuffy room.

"I'm Dr. Lamas. It's good to meet you," I said. "The way this clinic works is that we talk about what's going on and I'll ask you some questions, and then I'll examine you and we'll talk about transplant and see if moving forward with the evaluation is the right thing for you."

She nodded.

I asked her to tell me her story. Though I had just read through her notes, I preferred to hear it from her. She hesitated—telling it might take a while, and she didn't want to use up too much time—but I assured her that she should go ahead. We weren't in a rush. So she took a deep breath and started to talk. She told me about the cough, the visits to doctor after doctor; the misdiagnoses of asthma, reflux, and allergies; the inhalers, the pills, and the oxygen; and finally the diagnosis of pulmonary fibrosis that had landed her here. As she was talking I listened, asked questions, nodded and typed. Whatever I wrote would follow my patient in her medical record, copied forward from note to note, perhaps forever. I would try to get it right.

"So, do you think I need a transplant?" she asked me.

Even though she had been on oxygen for years, and she could see the dial cranking up and feel her strength winding down, the entire idea of being evaluated for a lung transplant must have still sounded preposterous. Perhaps she hoped that I would take one look at her and tell her that she didn't belong there at all, and that she should come back when she was actually sick. But instead I told her that for people with her disease, we generally recommend starting an evaluation for transplant as early as possible. So the answer was yes, she would likely need a transplant. Even though she didn't need it right now, she might in the future, and her doctors had done the right thing in sending her to our clinic. "With your disease, your lungs could fail quickly, and we don't want to get caught in a situation where we have waited too long," I explained.

"Oh," she replied.

"What other questions can I answer?" I asked.

I thought she might want to know what would happen if she never got a transplant, and if she did get new lungs, whether she would be able to tolerate the surgery, and what her life would be like afterward. Or maybe she was wondering whether her husband would be able to take care of her without resenting her disease or, worse yet, resenting her for having it. Perhaps she was thinking about the house, and how they would be able to keep it if her husband had to leave work; or if it was too early to tell her children what was going on, and when she did tell them, how she would be able to do that without pressuring them to drop everything in their lives and come to Boston. Later on, when she understood more about the course her disease might take, she might want to know about the limbo of ventilator dependence, whether she would regret her decisions if that's how things ended up, whether she'd be angry. I imagined that even though she wished I could answer those questions for her, it all felt unbelievable, so far away. She was just at the beginning. So she said no—thank you, no more questions right now.

We moved forward. Regardless of what choices she would ultimately make, this was the only direction we could go. I helped her up onto the examining table. She slowly unbuttoned her shirt so that I could place my stethoscope on her back to listen to her lungs. I noticed as she unbuttoned that the skin on her chest was smooth and unmarred by the scars of surgery. I held and inspected her hands, recording the way that years of low oxygen had left her nails curved and misshapen. I traced the shape with my fingers. I pushed up her pants to feel her shins for swelling, and palpated the joints of her arms and legs. Then I sat back down. There was nothing in her exam or her file that should keep her from moving forward with the evaluation. She wasn't obese, she wasn't hooked on narcotics or high-dose steroids. And she had an incurable lung disease. I told her that she would need to bring three people with her for an hour-long meeting when she came to the hospital overnight for all the tests. These people would make up her support team. She told me this wouldn't be a problem.

Then I was done. It would take time to grow accustomed to this part of my job. I left the room to review my patient's history with the pre-transplant nurse who would be her point person moving forward. She was smart, funny, and kind, and I knew my patient was lucky to have her. She would schedule all the necessary testing. Quite possibly, I would never see this patient again. My role was just to meet her this one time, at the gates, to lay the foundation before she launched into the unknown.

Shortly after my first session in the transplant evaluation clinic, I started my attending rotation at Spaulding, the long-term hospital where I had first met Charlie Atkinson. The Spaulding shifts are less sought after than those in the intensive care unit, so they are often given to first-year attending doctors like me. Spaulding is a good place for a writer to gather stories, that much I knew. But I suspected that it would also be a rich place for a doctor to better understand the limits of prognostication, to see what life actually looks like for patients who have not died but are not yet truly better, either: these survivors in the middle.

I had grown used to walking those halls as an observer and writer, so it felt a bit strange, that first day, to enter

Spaulding as a doctor. It was familiar, but in a way it was foreign, too. I printed my patient list and began my morning rounds. A sign on my first patient's door said that I had to wear a mask and a yellow gown to enter, so I dutifully donned the protective gear. I knocked—which I would later learn drove my patient crazy, since she was on the ventilator in the morning and as a result couldn't make herself heard even if she didn't want someone to enter—and was met with silence, so I stepped in. Cards covered the walls like wallpaper. My patient, a woman in her early twenties, sat in a chair next to the bed in shorts and a T-shirt, with her thinning hair done up in two braids.

"You don't have to wear the mask," she mouthed, after my introduction. Even though her tracheostomy tube was connected to the ventilator, rendering her voiceless, I was relieved to find that I could easily read her lips. "Unless you have a hacking cough or, I don't know, are planning to lick me or something."

I smiled. "Probably not," I said.

I placed my stethoscope on her chest, listened to the air move in and out of her scarred lungs, and confirmed that she would try to breathe without the vent later that day, as she did each day with intermittent success during her physical therapy session. Then I checked her name off my list. I had nearly thirty patients to see. On the first day, all I could do was get to know a little bit about each of them.

My roster included a gentle, childlike older woman who was on too much oxygen to be able to go home, and who spent her days working diligently on adult coloring books. Her roommate on the other side of the curtain was a sarcastic, highly anxious New Yorker with lung cancer whose darting eyes and grimace made clear that she was furious she wouldn't be able to talk until we removed her tracheostomy tube. Down the hall from them, an obese man whose obstructive sleep apnea left him hooked to a ventilator at night told me that I was beautiful like a movie star and asked me each morning whether I was married ("Still not married," I said, long after it had stopped being funny).

There were also patients who couldn't interact in a way that I could understand at all, those who had suffered major brain injuries or who were profoundly delirious as a result of recurrent infections. Some of these people had family members who visited every day and sat by the bedside; others spent their time locked in endless solitude. One ventilator-dependent woman had turned eighty-five there, in her room at the end of the hall. She had been transferred from a rehab hospital that had closed down, and she was never going to be able to go home. Likely, there was no longer any home for her outside these walls. She passed the time doing electronic jigsaw puzzles, with an occasional visit from her son or a trip outdoors once every few weeks when the respiratory therapists had time to take her. Even on my lightning-fast rounds through my patient list that first day, I think I knew that if I let myself feel deeply for each of them I might drown. I definitely would never get to finish my notes.

But the young woman I saw first drew me in. She spent around six hours each day off the ventilator, and during that time I could hear her voice. It struck me as a cruel irony that such a talker spent so much of her day unable to make a sound. I liked listening to her. She made me laugh with her candid, perceptive observations about the other doctors and nurses and with stories like the one about the running bet she'd had with her mother over whether she could get a particularly serious doctor to crack a smile. (It had taken months, but she'd succeeded. After all that, she couldn't remember precisely how.) I spent more time in her room than I had to, and as the days passed she told me her story. She had been a college student who felt kind of run-down and assumed she had a cold or maybe mono, which turned out not to be a cold at all, but acute leukemia. She had to leave school to get started on urgent chemotherapy. She had gone into remission, even returned to school, thinking things might be okay after all, but she had relapsed some months later. Now, more than five years had passed, and her cancer was gone. She'd been cured of her leukemia, but she was left with a progressive lung disease as a long-term side effect of her successful treatment.

"Pretty crazy, huh?" she asked. I nodded. I didn't know what to do with stories like these, other than to shake my head and begin to worry that each cough meant I had lung cancer or each freckle on my leg was actually an early melanoma. "There's a lot more to it. Those are just the bullet points," she told me. "But it's still more than you'd get from the chart."

It was. I asked her how she spent her time. She responded that she had tried it all. There had been a Netflix period, but she'd tired of that. She surfed the Internet, looked at what her friends were up to on Facebook, and when she was feeling better, she had even gone through a knitting kick. She was running out of ideas. Often, when I came into the room I found her sitting on her chair, looking at her phone or out the window, daydreaming. A few of her close friends visited from time to time, and if she was off the vent she talked with them as much as her breath allowed. Otherwise she mouthed and gestured so they could understand. A week before I met her, she had been able to go outside, for the first time in months. She and her physical therapist had walked down the street to a medical supply store to try out new rolling walkers. It was exhausting, but good.

One morning, when I came in on my daily rounds, she asked me a question. She wanted to know if she was on life support. The question took me by surprise and I paused behind my mask. I wondered if she would say more, if she would ask me what that meant and whether she would ever get home, and I would have to tell her that I hoped so but couldn't promise it. She was quiet, though, so I replied, "Well, you need the ventilator, which is a form of life support. So I would say so.... Why do you ask?"

She gave a small shrug. "I was just wondering, but that's what I thought," she mouthed. "I'm connected to life support through the hole in my neck."

She then shifted her body forward in her chair and

pulled up the back of her T-shirt so that I could examine her as usual. I felt her question and the weight of its meaning sit there, heavy and silent, as I placed my stethoscope on her back and listened to the quiet sounds of her breath.

On a Friday evening a few days later, I came in to tell her about a small change we were making to her ventilator settings for the night and found that her room had been turned into an Indian buffet. Her parents were there along with one of her friends, and I hesitated in the doorway. Ideally, I'd let them eat and come back, but it was already getting late.

My patient looked in my direction, beckoning me into the room.

"Help yourself," her mother said, and offered me a plate. I shook my head, explaining that I just needed to update my patient about the ventilator settings. I would be quick. "We're planning to go up a little on the pressure on your vent tonight," I told her. We hoped this might help her spend more time off the vent during the day. She nodded, clearly distracted, and then gestured to the food and mouthed, "Okay. Have some."

I paused. I have never been sure of the protocol in these situations. As I hesitated, I found myself listening to the familiar sighing sound of my patient's ventilator. I could still hear it in the background despite the dinnertime chatter. Thinking about life support, about the question my patient had asked me that recent morning, and all the many questions she had not asked, I took the plate. "Thank you," I replied.

I lowered my mask to have a bite. It was the first time I had breathed comfortably in that room. The food was warm and spicy. I stood against the wall with my mask around my neck, surprised by how nice it all felt and hoping I hadn't spent too long interrupting their dinner, before I said good-night.

Back in transplant clinic a few weeks later, I was walking through the waiting room to see my first patient of the day when a young woman in a wheelchair stopped in front of me. She had short hair and big hoop earrings and was neatly put together in a silky blouse and dress pants. I didn't know who she was at first, but when she spoke I recognized her voice immediately. She was a woman I had first met in the hospital some months back, when she was waiting for a transplant. At the time I had talked with her a bit about what it was like to live while wait-ing. She told me that she watched a lot of television, tried to read but couldn't focus, and that her mother sat at her bedside every day, leaving only to buy her cards and trinkets from the hospital gift shop. At first she didn't seem to mind my being there, so I fell into the habit of stopping by every now and again, mostly in the after-noon or evening, just to sit in her room and hope that she might tell me more about her experience. But as the weeks passed without a transplant she grew more withdrawn and less animated. I began to worry that I was burdening her with my presence, and my visits became less frequent. Then, a surprise—one spring morning the surgeons entered her room with the news. Lungs.

I heard about her transplant through the hospital grapevine, and though I thought of her occasionally, I didn't see her after the surgery. Months later, on an overnight shift in the ICU, I noticed her name on my list of patients. She'd received the new lungs, had made it out of the hospital and to rehab, but now was intubated and battling a new infection. That night I stood at her bedside. She was sedated to the point of unconsciousness, paralyzed to allow the ventilator to do its work. Her body was swollen and still. I thought of those months of waiting and remembered her mother, the way she sat in the corner of her daughter's hospital room, offering a sad smile and a tired greeting to the doctors and nurses who passed in and out. I tinkered with my patient's ventilator settings throughout the night and titrated the medications to support her blood pressure. When I left the hospital in the morning, I never expected to see her again.

But there she was, sitting in the waiting room of the clinic with her mother at her side, as before. She was wearing a mask to protect her compromised immune system from the threat of infection, but I thought I could make out the shadow of a smile behind it and I grinned back at her. "How are you?" I asked.

"All my hair fell out," she told me, gesturing self-consciously at her close-cropped hair. I had thought the cut was intentional, fashionable. "It must have been one of the medicines. It's growing back now."

She had been admitted again a handful of times since she'd left the ICU and was still too weak to walk, she told me. She struggled with persistent nausea and panicked each time she entered the hospital, even for scheduled appointments. But she was home. And maybe she would continue to get better and her hospital admissions would grow fewer, the time at home longer. On the other hand, maybe what I saw before me that day was as good as it would get for her. Perhaps I would next encounter her overnight, back in the intensive care unit. Her body could reject her transplanted lungs or finally succumb to a disseminated infection it couldn't fight. She might never exit what I perceived as limbo to emerge, fully healed, on the other side.

There was so much I wanted to know from her—first, what it had been like to live in the hospital while hoping for lungs that might never come, and now, what it was like to be alive and to reenter the world after a survival that had come at such a high cost. But at that moment, she was living at home with the immediate threat of critical illness lifted, however briefly. And she wanted to say hello and to share the strange thing that had happened to her hair.

"Well, I like the hair," I said, honestly. I was tempted to stay and talk more, but I had a full clinic schedule. "You know, I'm so happy I ran into you," I told her. I picked up the pile of medical records and CT scan reports for the people I'd see in clinic that afternoon. There was a lot to read. Then I looked over my shoulder, pausing for just a moment to watch as my patient's mother wheeled her out of the clinic office, beyond my line of sight, and into the sun of a summer afternoon.

Afterword

This is not a book about death, though death is present in these pages, an unavoidable reality in the background of each diagnosis and decision. Even with the VAD, there is death. Even with ventilators, ECMO, infection control in cystic fibrosis, even with transplantation and electric shocks, the outcome is ultimately the same.

But this is a book about life. It's a book about how people live today, both in the shadow of and enabled by previously inconceivable advances. In a way, it's a hopeful book, although that's not what I expected at the start. When I began, I knew I wanted to find people who were alive, maybe for days or maybe for years, as a result of today's medical interventions, and I wanted to learn more about what their lives were like. I started out with an assumption that I might encounter people who were miserable in modern-day purgatory, men and women whose lives had been extended against their wills, who would perhaps prefer for their suffering to have ended. But that's not all I found. Through Facebook messages, an illicit summer fishing trip, or a carefully assembled sandwich, the people in this book move forward even as their days diminish, finding meaning in lives that are nothing like what they had planned.

As we look toward our futures, we may each be faced with new machines and life-prolonging possibilities, all with different costs and consequences. When it comes time to weigh these choices, there will be no clear right or wrong. I can only hope that the stories captured in these pages, and in the brief updates here, might help us to enter and navigate our ways through these new worlds with our eyes open.

In Cambridge, Massachusetts, it is Charlie Atkinson's coda. He celebrated his eightieth with a fantastic party held at the Harvard men's club he had belonged to as an undergraduate. It was a swanky event, perfectly executed by Jeannette, the kind I never would have been invited to if I hadn't walked into Charlie's room that day at the long-term acute care hospital. The wine flowed and the guests snacked on cheese and crackers before heading upstairs to a birthday dinner and toasts. I saw a few familiar faces from the rehab hospital, including the physical therapist who had taken Charlie into her boot camp and pushed him to get moving again, but most of the assembled crowd had nothing to do with sickness. Charlie was clearly the man of the evening, wearing a tux, a white tie, and a top hat. His voice, once muted by the trach tube, boomed as he made his way through the crowd, leaning over his walker to meet and greet. Despite the chronic urinary catheter and nerve pain and weakness he carries with him, Charlie is alive, and he is still getting better. At eighty years old, he is making plans for the future. He has started a new company that aims to create what Charlie calls the "Atkinson artificial mind." He's fundraising, hiring, building a website, and contemplating writing a book, all while helping to plan his upcoming Harvard College Class of 1958 sixtieth reunion. His are big, ambitious plans, the kind that are generally reserved for younger men, and all of that feels good.

Van Chauvin continued to enjoy his freedom after coming off the transplant list. He was able to switch most of his care back to doctors near his home—a change that meant fewer days spent navigating traffic and waiting in offices, and more time, energy, and battery power for the activities he enjoyed. In our conversations throughout the spring and early summer after we met, we did not talk about hospitals and transplants; instead, Van told me about his plans with his family, his excitement over a new grandchild on the way, things he dreamed he might build.

But this past August, in the waning days of a Massachusetts summer, Van Chauvin died. When I learned of his death by email a few days after it happened, I found myself replaying our many phone calls. The last time we talked, about a month before his death, Van had invited me to spend an afternoon with him on his boat. I had

smiled, thinking—despite all I knew about average life expectancies and the realities of the VAD—that there might
be time.

Though I know now that I'll never have the chance to
see Van out there in his element, this is how I will choose
to remember him. I won't think of him in the clinic office,
but instead, I'll imagine him on the lake with his fishing
pole, battery packs slung over his shoulders as he waits for
a nibble and then reels in a fish, throwing caution to the
wind to enjoy a simple moment of pleasure.

It has been eleven years since Nancy Andrews's surgery and
its aftermath, and while her delirium-inspired sketches continue to make their way through the world, she has moved
on to other themes. She recently created a set of sculptures
that she describes as "accidents"—unrecognizable bodies,
strange and twisted. In a Web series titled *The Strange Eyes
of Dr. Myes*, she tells the story of a scientist and researcher
who tries to re-create the deep sense of connection to others that she felt during a near-death experience. She has
also returned to making her own music these days and is
learning the ukulele and tenor guitar.

But the consequences of critical illness haven't left her.
Perhaps it was her time in the intensive care unit, perhaps
it is having a genetic disorder that can cause her vessels to
tear or her retinas to detach, but Nancy often finds herself
considering her own mortality. She wonders, too, about the
long-term effects of post-traumatic stress disorder. Noise

and chaos spark an intense anxiety within her—is this because of the delirium she experienced while in the unit?

She will never be entirely free of the hospital and the burdens of her diagnosis. During a recent phone call, she mentioned in passing that she needed to schedule her regular two-to-three-year follow-up with her Boston doctors. She worries less about this than she did when she was younger, but still, returning to the hospital reminds her of being delirious, terrified, and out of control. And yet, she will call and make the appointment. She will submit her body to the CT scanner and to whatever comes next. Then, hopefully, she will return home cleared for another few years. "It's like going back to the belly of the beast," she told me. "But you just have to keep facing it."

I continue to follow Ben Clancy's progress intermittently through his mother's Facebook updates. When I last spoke with Andrea, about six months had passed since I had observed Ben's outpatient therapy and more than a year since the overdose. I was curious to hear how far he had come. He had recently struggled with pneumonia, I learned, and he wasn't talking as much as he had been before that setback. His doctors had scheduled a CT scan of his head just to make sure nothing else was going on, and his therapy was on hold until they could get that done. With our earlier conversations in mind, I asked Andrea again what she thought about the future and how much progress she could hope for.

She knows Ben won't ever be the same as the son she

had before the accident, but...how far will he come? She can't let that line of thought consume her. For now, Ben has returned to his old habit of spending an hour each day with Reuters news online, and he seems engaged by that in the moment, though afterward he doesn't remember what he read. Andrea found someone to play guitar with Ben each week, and although it's more classic rock than the jazz Ben used to prefer, he still remembers his chords, and appears to enjoy the music. Not one to rest, Andrea has also been working on the possibility of a service dog to help Ben with his balance. And there is another summer around the bend, and an e-mail she just received from the Montessori school Ben attended when he was younger, asking if he might want to spend some time there. Maybe she and Ben could do work in the garden. So yes, Andrea wonders about the future, she said. "But it doesn't matter today, does it?"

Cindy Scribner hasn't been hospitalized again. There are doctors' appointments and medications and lab tests, but it has been three years since her transplant, and the fear that she is rejecting her new lungs has faded. Though her life has taken a different shape, she still misses her work as a nurse. She knows now that she'll never be able to return to that job—her immune system is too fragile—but Cindy continues to hope she can find a different kind of work that helps pay the bills and feels meaningful. Until then, she keeps busy with her family. After all that has happened, the normalcy of these regular days is like a miracle.

* * *

In the months after Eddie Beatrice got his transplant, the media was all over him with profiles in the local paper and TV stations. Most of the press was positive, or at least lightheartedly curious, but there were those who criticized him for taking his need into his own hands, promoting himself and in doing so "cutting the line." This hurt him, because all he wanted was to be able to get back to the person he had been before the shoulder surgery, and Kelly gave him that chance by offering him a kidney on Facebook.

Now the coverage has died down. And in many ways, Eddie is back on the path that was interrupted so many years ago by his surgery and kidney failure. His children have both graduated from college. His wife is "still beautiful inside and out." Eddie isn't sure how he would have survived it all without her. Work is going well—so well, in fact, that Eddie's great performance recently won him and his wife a trip for two to Turks and Caicos. But in the background of it all, Eddie is "constantly and forever" heading to the hospital to get his labs checked and meet with doctors. His transplanted kidney took a back seat to a new health scare recently when testing revealed that he had prostate cancer. After a period of watching and waiting, and blood tests and biopsies, his doctors decided to remove the organ. Eddie was at home recovering after his prostate surgery when we last talked, and I was relieved to hear the good news that the cancer hadn't spread.

He and Kelly still keep in touch, and made sure to spend some time catching up during a recent trip Eddie and his wife took to California. As for the kidney, it's doing well, allowing Eddie to continue with the work of living his life.

Meghan and Myles had a great time in Mexico. But a few months after they returned home, Meghan got sick again. Sometimes she can feel it coming, and she knows she'll end up in the hospital, tied to that intravenous line for antibiotics. But this time it surprised her. One day she was feeling strong enough to take a spin class, and the next she was in the ER with a drop in her lung function and plans for an admission. It was the start of the school year, and all she could think was that she'd left her students in the lurch. Her colleagues pitched in and everything worked out, but maybe this would be the catalyst for Meghan to start easing her family and friends into the idea that she'll slow down and ultimately stop working one day. With the increasing amount of time she must spend on the task of staying as healthy as possible, she finds herself quite simply running out of hours, and she wants those in her life to be prepared so they don't assume she's on her deathbed when she does decide to leave her job.

Saying the words aloud helps her, too. It doesn't sound so bad. Maybe she'll retire before she turns forty, and that will be okay. And she is realizing that it will be okay, too, if she and Myles don't get pregnant, if they don't adopt. When she's healthy, it is so easy to imagine working for decades more and having a baby, but then she's in the hospital again, and it feels improbable, even irresponsible, to consider having a child. Her medical needs require so much time. And what happens when, inevitably, she gets sick?

So Meghan reminds herself that her life is good as it is. She gets to come home to Myles every night. They have a beautiful house, close family and friends, and Myles makes her laugh. They can plan great trips for as long as Meghan is able to take them. And they are busy. Meghan recently organized a spin class fundraiser for the CF Foundation, she is planning a vegetable garden, and she and Myles are hoping to get a new dog. "We have so many positive things," Meghan told me. "If the family thing isn't the direction for Myles and me, then, well, that's going to have to be fine."

As for me, I have my transplant evaluation clinic and my rotations at Spaulding, but most of my time in the ICU takes place overnight. That's just the way it is for me now, and I struggle with the lack of continuity inherent in caring for critically ill people only one night at a time, when the sun goes down. It's an odd dynamic: twelve intense hours of life and death like a strange dream while the world is asleep, and then, in the morning, it is over, the decisions belong to someone else, and I emerge, tired and hungry. In a way, there is little time in all of this to think about the before and the after. Yet I try to bring some of what I've learned from the people in these pages into my daily work.

We recently started a peer support group for ICU survivors and their families. We've met on a few Saturday
mornings: an ICU social worker, a psychiatrist, another
critical care physician, and me. Over pastries and coffee,
I listen to men and women admit that even though their
spouses are alive and home and they know they should be
happy, they wake to the phantom sounds of hospital alarms
or burst into tears without warning. Patients tell me how
they still remember being tied down to a bed, pulling out
intravenous lines, struggling to communicate. These stories no longer surprise me. But even within the familiar
themes, there is what feels like an infinite variety, and I
continue to learn.

We're still building our clinic. It's small, but it is growing.
Some of our patients tell us that they are doing "okay" as
they slowly reenter their lives, and when they do, I try to
remember to pause and to ask them about that word. The
answers vary. For some, being okay means that their thinking is intact and that they are able to sleep comfortably,
despite trach tubes or home ventilators or lists upon lists of
medications. For others, it is being back at work or at the
gym, strong enough to care for their families.

There are also patients who tell us that though they're
back home, they don't have the mental fortitude to return
to their prior jobs. They startle easily during the day, or
they wake in the middle of the night in a sweat. The ICU
was hell, and they have emerged only to find that they
are still in limbo and they don't recognize themselves any

longer. We tell them they are not crazy. We give them a diagnosis—post–intensive care syndrome—and we are honest about the realities when we say that we might not be able to fix it, but that we can listen.

I accompanied one woman back upstairs to the intensive care unit where she'd spent nearly two weeks intubated and sedated. She did not remember the place but she knew her room number, so we walked slowly into the unit and stood in front of the room that had been hers. The curtain was closed. There was a patient in the bed. I watched her face as she waited for a flash of familiarity that did not come. "Are you all right?" I asked. I worried she would feel let down. She didn't recognize any of the doctors or nurses, and no one recognized her. There was no applause. It wasn't the triumphant return I had imagined. But she wasn't disappointed, she told me. Instead, she was relieved. This was just a place. I tried to see it through her eyes—smaller than she'd assumed, less threatening, too. She could enter, this time by choice. And then she could leave.

In a way, I, too, am still navigating unfamiliar territory. I have spent the entirety of my medical training with a narrow focus on clearly defined outcomes, such as days on the ventilator, readmissions, and, ultimately, mortality. These are necessary starting points. But the stories in this book have helped me to see that that's not all there is. A walk through an intensive care unit, a conversation over coffee at a support group, or a clinic visit to a doctor who can explain what happened to you in the ICU has real value, even if that value is something we don't yet know how to measure. As we continue to usher men and women toward the uncertain worlds that lie beyond survival, it is a start.

It has been nearly ten years since that intern year winter, when I pulled a central line from a young man's neck and responded to his Facebook friend request. In a way, I think, the entirety of this book grew out of that exchange. The details have changed a little in this retelling, I'm sure, as memory fades and distorts, but the essential pieces remain. And I find that I'm still not sure what I would do if I could return to that bedside, that winter day in the ICU. Maybe I should have ignored the request altogether. That undoubtedly would have been more professional. But even now, years later, there is a greater part of me that wishes I still had the chance to reply. "Yes," I could have written. It would have been a simple message. "You can stop humming now."

Acknowledgments

The path to becoming a doctor is relatively clear; the path to becoming a writer, less so.

For showing me the way, thank you to my agent and friend, Lorin Rees. Lorin first reached out to me by e-mail a few years ago, after reading a piece I had published in the *New York Times*. Through his skill and advocacy, I've had the opportunity to work with Tracy Behar, Ian Straus, Peggy Freudenthal, and the staff at Little, Brown. Together, this team has helped me turn what still feels a little like fantasy into something real.

I would also like to acknowledge my friends and colleagues at Brigham and Women's Hospital, Ariadne Labs, and the Spaulding Hospital for Continuing Medical Care for their encouragement throughout this process. Bruce Levy and Gerald Weinhouse have helped me create a home for my interests in the Brigham's pulmonary and critical care division. I have been extremely lucky to benefit from a fantastic mentor, Susan Block, without whom I never would have had the research or clinical experience that ultimately led to this book. I have also enjoyed the uniquely good fortune to learn from one of my heroes, Atul Gawande, whose work inspires me to become a better doctor and thinker.

Thank you to Emily for her red pen and red lines, her patience throughout this project, her enthusiasm and, always, support.

To my brother, who fascinates me with the nonmedical career he has chosen, and who never fails to make me laugh. To my father, who instilled in me an early love of medicine, and has served as my unofficial overnight cardiology consult and medical fact checker, far too many times to count. I would not have become a doctor without his influence.

Most of all, I thank my greatest fan and first editor— my mother. For as long as I can remember, she has been my champion, encouraging me to "reach for the stars and beyond." Her pride, unconditional love, and unwavering belief in me mean more than I can ever say. This book is for her.

Finally, my deep gratitude goes to the patients who allowed me into their lives and shared their stories. Thank you. It has been an honor.

About the Author

Daniela Lamas is a pulmonary and critical care doctor at Brigham and Women's Hospital and is on the faculty at Harvard Medical School. Following graduation from Harvard College, she went on to earn her MD at Columbia College of Physicians and Surgeons, where she also completed her internship and residency. She then returned to Boston for her subspecialty fellowship. She has worked as a medical reporter at the *Miami Herald* and is frequently published in the *New York Times*. This is her first book.